THE WAKEFiELD WAY

a 75-mile walking route around the Wakefield Metropolitan District

by

Douglas Cossar

The Ramblers

Other publications by the Ramblers' Association (West Riding Area)
Dales Way Handbook (with the Dales Way Association, annually)
Douglas Cossar, *Ramblers' Leeds,* 2nd edition,
Volume 1 East of Leeds (1999)
Douglas Cossar, *Ramblers' Leeds,* 2nd edition,
Volume 2 West of Leeds (2000)
Douglas Cossar, *The Airedale Way* (1996)
Douglas Cossar, *Ramblers' Wakefield* (1997)
Marje Wilson, *The Brontë Way* (1997)
Douglas Cossar, *Ramblers' Bradford,* Volume 1 (1999)
Douglas Cossar & John Lieberg, *Country Walks in Mirfield, Emley,
Thornhill and Denby Dale* (2002)

RAMBLERS' ASSOCIATION (WEST RIDING AREA)
27 Cookridge Avenue, Leeds LS16 7NA

ISBN 1 901184 74 9

Cover photographs
<u>Front:</u> Old bridge over the River Dearne, Bretton Park.
<u>Back:</u> Emroyd Common, railway viaduct at Horbury Bridge, old boat
moored by lock-keeper's cottage.

Publishers' Note
At the time of publication all footpaths used in these walks were
designated as public rights of way or permissive footpaths, or were paths
over which access has traditionally not been denied, but it should be
borne in mind that diversion orders may be made or permissions
removed. Although every care has been taken in the preparation of this
guide, neither the author nor the publisher can accept responsibility for
those who stray from the routes described.

Printed and bound by Hart & Clough Ltd., Cleckheaton, West Yorkshire.

Contents

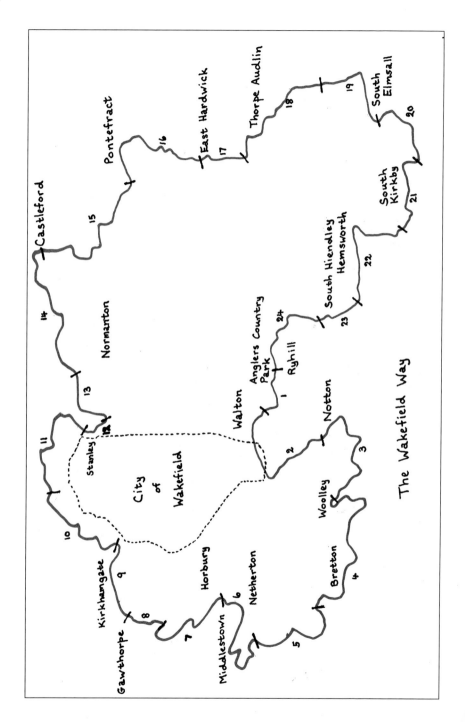

The Wakefield Way

4

Author's Note

To those who are not familiar with it the variety and attractiveness of the countryside around Wakefield may come as something of a surprise. Of course there are relics of the onetime coal mining industry, but industrial railways are now quiet walkways and spoil heaps are now grassy hills or country parks. There are large, prosperous arable fields in the east, undulating Pennine pastures in the west, country estates like Walton Hall and Bretton Hall, much woodland and charming villages. Lots to delight the walker.

Some years ago, when I was preparing my *Ramblers' Wakefield*, it seemed to me a pity that a city of Wakefield's importance did not have its "Boundary Walk" or its "Country Way" or its "Ringway", and I sketched out a possible route. But as is the way with such projects, nothing came of it until the Wakefield Group of the Ramblers' Association became interested and did some preliminary exploration. But again the project ran out of steam, and it was passed back to me. Here now, seven years after *Ramblers' Wakefield,* is my suggested route. I am grateful to the Wakefield Group for all their work and ideas, but for better or for worse the final choice of route is mine and reflects my own tastes in walking.

There will be those who do the Way as a long-distance linear walk, but I am sure that there are many more, not so serious ramblers, who will prefer to collect it in sections over a longer period of time. For them I have divided the route up into 24 sections, 21 of which have been made into circular walks; the other three, linear walks, are well served by public transport. All the walks use public rights of way or permissive paths or paths where no one is likely to object.

Three Ordnance Survey Explorer maps cover the route, numbers 278 Sheffield and Barnsley, 288 Bradford and Huddersfield and 289 Leeds. Once more I am grateful to the Ordnance Survey for permission to base my very primitive sketch maps on these Explorers. All maps are reproduced by permission of Ordnance Survey (based mapping) on behalf of The Controller of Her Majesty's Stationery Office, © Crown Copyright 100033886. My maps are greatly simplified and are intended simply to give a general overview of the course of the walk: they should on no account be used as guides to navigation!

Please read the route descriptions carefully: I have tried to make them clear and unambiguous and to eliminate the risk of misinterpretation. But in my experience people sometimes go astray through not concentrating on the text of a walk, inadvertently skipping a line or jumping by mistake from one stile to the next, or just losing the place through being engrossed in conversation with their companions! The route of the Wakefield Way is printed in **bold,** background material in *italic.*

I hope that no difficulties will be encountered *en route.* If you should encounter any obstacles, nuisances or other difficulties, please report them to the Public Rights of Way Section, Wakefield MDC, Newton Bar, Wakefield WF1 2TX (01924-306090). In summer dense undergrowth may make some paths into semi-jungle experiences, and there are the odd stiles which need attention. Do look out for the occasional bull at large in pastures in the summer months and take suitable evasive action, even if this means a minor trespass. Better safe than sorry! Frisky young cattle and horses may give you unwelcome attention, particularly if you have a dog, but are rarely dangerous.

All the walks are accessible by public transport, and I have given details as they are known to me at the moment. But please do check this information with West Yorkshire Metro (0113-245-7676).

I am particularly grateful for the help and advice of Trevor Hiles, Footpath Secretary of the R.A.'s Wakefield Group, in the preparation of this book. His comments and suggestions have been invaluable, and he has provided all the photographs used in the book.

In the last resort responsibility for any mistakes or inadequacies is mine alone.

A waymark specific to the Wakefield Way has been designed (it is illustrated on the front cover), and it is hoped that the whole route will be waymarked in the near future.

Happy walking!

Douglas Cossar
November 2004

Walk 1
Anglers Country Park and the Heronry

Walk length 4.5 miles (7.25 km), of which 1.86 miles (3 km) is Wakefield Way. An easy stroll through woodland and by the Barnsley Canal is followed by an exploration of the grounds of the former Walton Hall. The Wakefield Way starts from Anglers Country Park close to the village of Wintersett. Here are to be found an ample free car park, the Waterton Countryside Discovery Centre (opening times vary), Squire's Café (open daily 10-5 in summer, restricted in the winter) and toilets, as well as a glorious country park and lakeside nature reserve. Anglers Country Park, created from a former opencast mining site and opened in 1986, includes a 30 hectare lake, is rich in wildlife and provides one of the most important over-wintering bird sites in West Yorkshire. Leaflets with more information about Squire Waterton and the Heronry can be obtained from the Discovery Centre.

By bus: 195/196 Wakefield-Ryhill-Hemsworth, 197 Wakefield-Ryhill-Newstead to Wintersett; continue on foot through the village, and after leaving it take the first minor road on the right, Haw Park Lane, signposted to Anglers Country Park, and follow it to the main car-park.

By car: The Heronry and the Waterton Countryside Discovery Centre are well signposted from surrounding roads. The car-park is on Haw Park Lane (GR 375 153).

From the car park, return to the road and turn right, ignoring immediately a turn on the left into the West Riding Sailing Club, *which uses Wintersett Reservoir, which was built in 1854 originally to supply water to the Barnsley Canal.* **When you reach a fork, ignore the unsurfaced track on the left, pass round the gate and continue along the tarmac lane. Soon the tarmac runs out and the track emerges between open fields with Haw Park Wood straight ahead. Enter the wood via a stile alongside a metal gate. 50 yards beyond is a display board and signpost. Take the track straight ahead signposted Walton North Trans-Pennine Trail, but when the wall of the former Walton Park Estate appears ahead, fork left 20 yards before it. Ignore a footpath and then a track forking left (the latter marking the yellow circuit) and you will reach a large open space where several tracks converge.** *Notice the mediaeval knight carved from a tree stump on the right.*

Take the second right (signposted TPT-horses Walton North), but after 8 yards fork left down a narrow path between the trees. This

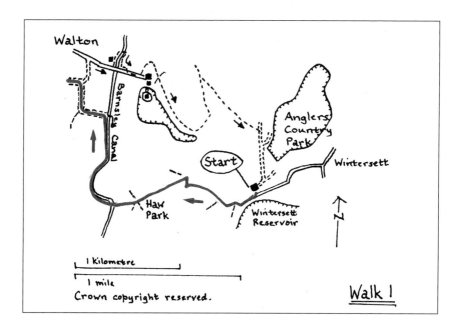

Crown copyright reserved.

descends steeply at first then more gradually, until having been joined by another path from the left you find yourself alongside the old Barnsley Canal, *opened in 1799 to carry coal from Barnsley and grain from Wakefield. Squire Waterton refused to allow the canal to go through his Park, instead, large cuttings had to be hewn out of the rock to the west of the estate, as we shall presently see. Today the disused waterway is a Site of Scientific Interest.* A little further on there are a few steps to help you up to the level of a wooden footbridge. *As you cross it, pause for a moment to look down at the old bridge supports and notice the grooves worn in the stonework by the towropes of the horse-drawn barges that used to ply this waterway.*

On the other side of the bridge turn right to walk along the towpath. *There is still some standing water in places, but much of the canal basin is now supporting a wide variety of flora and fauna.* Pass through one of the deep cuttings mentioned earlier and pass under a substantial stone bridge. Stay on the towpath for about another 100 yards, then double back up the embankment along a path signposted to Anglers Country Park, which passes through a small wood and reaches a roughly metalled track. Turn right. After a time the track turns right and becomes tarmac. At the next junction the Wakefield Way turns left, but we keep straight on. *[To continue with the route of the WW, jump to p. 12]*

At the top of the hill you enter Walton. At the next junction turn right along the access road to Waterton Park Golf Club and Waterton Park Hotel. Pass the entrance into the palatial clubhouse and a few yards further on fork right on a path which leads back down to the canal towpath. Turn sharp left along this, passing under a stone bridge. Ignore a wooden footbridge over the canal, pass a Trans-Pennine Trail Barnsley Canal information board and 80 yards further along turn right along a path which crosses the canal and passes through a doorway in the Walton Hall estate wall. *This stone wall, completed in 1824 to keep poachers out and wildlife in, stretched over 3 miles around the estate.* Take the path forking right and following the wall along. The quality of the path improves and you pass to the right of a putting green. The canal is over the wall on the right.

Bear left with the path, ignoring a few steps on the right up to the access road, pass the first tee and join the access road at the barrier and walk down it. There is a nice view of the rather undistinguished Walton Hall half right, *built in 1767 on the site of a manorial house where the Waterton family had lived for fourteen generations since 1453, with its lake beyond. Once just a moat around the house, the lake was enlarged by Waterton's father in 1790.* About 15 yards before the yellow striped speed hump turn left along a none too clear path through grass with bushes to the right and the golf course on the left. The path bears right and drops to a brick wall: turn left along this wall, in a few yards passing through a doorway in it. *The modern hotel buildings are visible to the right.* Follow the path through the rough grassland, dropping gently to a fence which leads in a few yards to a track.

Turn right. Where the fence on the right turns right and the track swings left over the golf course, turn right, pass to the right of a round water tank and climb through more long grass. Cross straight over a clear cross track which leads down right through a barrier to the new hotel, and continue on the path through the rough grassland. When you reach a golfers' buggy track cross straight over and walk up the path with a small wood on the right. Turn right at the top of the wood and follow the path back to the track. Keep forward along it. At the next junction keep straight on into the wood. When the track bears left, keep straight on along a narrower footpath. This is an attractive woodland path with the lake below on the right. At one point cross straight over a cross path.

Eventually the path emerges from the wood: the golf course is still on the left and the dilapidated estate wall once more to the right. Follow the wall along until you reach two stiles side by side just through the wall. Cross the right hand stile and walk back through the large field, bearing left away from the wall to the hedge on the far side, aiming for the spot where a hedge in the field beyond comes down the hillside. Cross the stile, footbridge, stile, and walk up the left hand edge of two fields. Cross two more stiles and turn right along the track. At the next junction turn left if you want to walk all the way round the lake, keep straight on otherwise. Further along on the right there is access to a nature reserve with a hide. At the next fork keep right. Shortly another track comes in from the left and the Discovery Centre can be seen ahead.

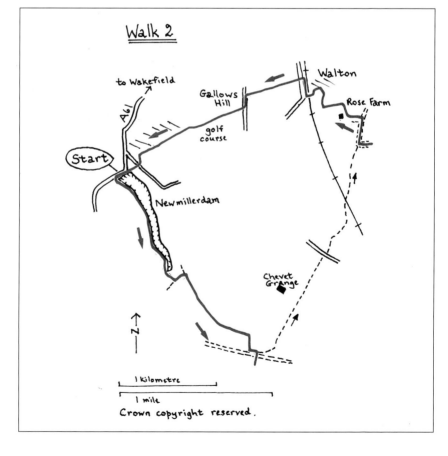

Walk 2

to Wakefield

A61

Gallows
Hill

golf
course

Walton

Rose Farm

Start

Newmillerdam

Chevet
Grange

N↑

I kilometre

I mile

Crown copyright reserved.

Walk 2
Walton and Newmillerdam

Length of walk 5.28 miles (8.5 km) of which 3.57 miles (5.75 km) is Wakefield Way. The wooded Newmillerdam Country Park is the highlight on this walk, with a variety of field paths to complete the circuit. There are good views from the 200 foot high Gallows Hill. The walk starts at the entrance to the Newmillerdam Country Park on the A61 Wakefield-Barnsley Road.

By bus: 58/59 Wakefield-Barnsley to Newmillerdam (half-hourly).

By car: Park either by the War Memorial (free, but small) or in the large pay-and-display car-park at the western end of the dam opposite the Fox and Hounds.

Take the lakeside path by the crenellated lodge between the pay-and-display car-park and the lake *and enjoy the vistas across the lake, the view of the recently restored Boathouse on the opposite shore (the first cornmill was probably built near here in 1285) and the opportunity to see a considerable bird population and, if you are lucky, other wildlife. The country park was once part of the mediaeval "Cevet" estate, which came into the ownership of the Pilkington family, who built the boathouse in the 1820s. The local authority acquired the park in 1954 and soon opened it up to the public.*

the Boathouse

Follow the lakeside path, after some time ignoring two paths to the left, one leading to a bridge across the lake as it narrows, the other over another bridge just beyond the far end of the lake. At this point keep straight on, ignoring a minor path forking right up into the woods. At the next fork take the left hand branch and then when you reach a T-junction of paths, where there is a bench, turn left again. Pass two stone gateposts and a bridge over a beck flowing into the lake, then ignoring the path going off left keep straight on for about 50 yards and turn right along the crossing path. Soon you

11

reach the end of the wood, and after passing over a stile by two more old stone gateposts with a barrier between, you find yourself out in open fields.

Head straight across the field and on the far side bear left with a beck to your right. A little further along you cross the beck by a stone footbridge, then turn left along its bank. About 100 yards short of some power lines, look out for a sharp turn to the right along a path which takes you directly up the hillside. When you reach the trees, take the wooden steps up to the left and then turn left along the path, which soon swings right over an old stone bridge. That's the onward route of the Wakefield Way, *[to continue with the route of the WW, jump to p.14]* but today we keep straight on. The path crosses a raised barrier and bends right to a second barrier. Fork left here along a narrow path which descends gently to the field edge. Turn sharp left and walk straight over the field.

On the far side bear right to cross the beck by a plank bridge, then walk along parallel to the hedge on the left until you find a gap in it with a bridge over the ditch. Cross this and turn left along the edge of the next field until you meet a cross wall. Turn right with this wall on your left and follow it all the way to where it bends left near Chevet Grange Farm. Here leave the wall and keep straight on along the field boundary to the next road. Cross diagonally right to a gap in the hedge opposite and walk along the enclosed path. At the end of the field cross the stile and continue along the right hand edge of the next field. At the end cross the stile and keep on to the corner of the next field, there turning left with the field edge. When you reach the remains of a stile in the remains of the fence on the right, fork right out of the field and drop to cross a railway by a bridge.

Bear left to a field and bear half left across the field to a large tree, then continue forward along the field boundary with the sparse remains of a hedge on your right. When you reach a tarmac lane, keep forward along it, **here re-joining the Wakefield Way, which comes up the track from the right. At the next junction turn left. Just before the buildings of Rose Farm the track turns right by a pond, then left by the corner of the farmhouse. At a gate into the farmyard, cross the stile into the field on your right and follow the path alongside the farm outbuildings - almost hidden among the grass are the remains of a path of stone flags.**

At the top left hand corner of the field cross a fence via a wooden stile, then immediately cross another stile onto the farm track and, almost opposite to the right, another wooden stile into another field. Head first for the pole supporting electricity cables (with Emley Moor TV mast visible on a clear day much further away behind it) **and then for**

another stile situated at the left extremity of the trees ahead. After this stile the path skirts the right edge of the field until, after yet another stile, you will see the houses of Walton village ahead. Keep to the right edge of the field all the way into the corner by the houses, then turn left parallel with the houses heading for a footbridge over the railway line - there's a wooden stile just before it.

You emerge via a stone stile into Common Lane. Cross the road and turn right for about 200 yards, with the buildings and spires of Wakefield in view ahead, until you see an obvious wall stile on your left and a path down to a stream, where it can be very muddy. The path crosses the stream by a wooden footbridge, then ascends through open fields, passing the remains of an old stone building and a pair of imposing stone gateposts and heading towards a telecommunications mast on the skyline. *This mast stands at Gallows Hill, at 200 feet above sea level one of the high points on this part of our route, with views of Walton to the rear, Wakefield to the right, Kettlethorpe, Crigglestone and Chapelthorpe ahead and the trees of Newmillerdam and Seckar Wood to the left.*

From the mast you emerge into Chevet Lane where you must cross over and turn left for about 90 yards to reach a wall stile on your right: cross into an open field and head along a path aiming towards the gap in the row of evergreen trees in the next field but one or just left of the Emley Moor mast if it is visible. The path passes into a golf course (Wakefield Golf Club). The way is indicated at first by two low green posts and after that you should aim for the left edge of a gap in the tall line of evergreen trees ahead. *Just check that no golfer is going to take a swing in your direction before you cross the fairways.* From the gap walk straight across the next fairway, through a patch of rough grass, then aim for a stile in the corner of a wooden fence straight ahead.

Cross the stile into a hedged path which you follow all the way to the houses of Newmillerdam, ignoring all points of access into the housing estate on the right. Walk down the tarmac drive and turn left at the bottom. Cross Hill Top Road, walk down some steps to the left of the long low building and descend steeply down Hill Road to return to your starting point. *[To continue with the route of the WW, jump back to p.11]*

Walk 3
Notton and Woolley

Length of walk 7.15 miles (11.5 km), of which 4.19 miles (6.75 km) is Wakefield Way. A pleasant route passing through arable land and woodland, with two attractive villages. The walk starts and finishes at the village green in Woolley. Woolley is mentioned as "Wolfeley" in the Domesday Book. The old name implies a forest glade frequented by wolves, and in fact two pits for trapping wolves have been found nearby. The village of today is one of the most attractive in the district. The old primary school next to Woolley village green has been converted into a community centre and the adjacent field into a play area, with benches, although there are no toilets.

By bus: 58 Wakefield-Barnsley (Mon-Sat hourly)

By car: Park beside the village green in Woolley near the village hall.

With your back to the entrance to the village hall turn left and walk along the road, crossing to the footway on the other side. Ignore Backhouse Lane on the left and shortly after you leave the village Parson Lane on the right. Follow Water Lane to its junction with Seckar Lane. Cross straight over and take the track opposite, which soon narrows to a footpath. Shortly an estate wall begins on the right. A little way along turn right through a broad gap in this wall, passing a barrier, and follow the broad path straight ahead, at first through heather and bracken, then descending through Seckar Wood. Follow it all the way to the A61 Wakefield-Barnsley road and turn right along the footway.

At the top of the hill, with Seckar Lane on the right, cross the main road and take the bridleway to the right of the entrance into the container depot. Follow it until you cross a disused railway track by a high bridge. On the far side of the bridge turn right and take a path which soon passes through a gap in a fence and follows a fence on the left down to the railway track. Bear left along it. After a time it runs along a high embankment with fields visible through the trees on both sides. About 200 yards before you reach the next bridge over the track a clear footpath comes up from the field on the left. A few yards further on fork left off the track on a path which climbs gently through the trees and runs parallel to the railway track.

After a time it drops slightly to the left and you reach a fork. The left branch drops into the field, but you keep right, in a few yards being joined by another path coming up from the left. **This is the Wakefield Way**

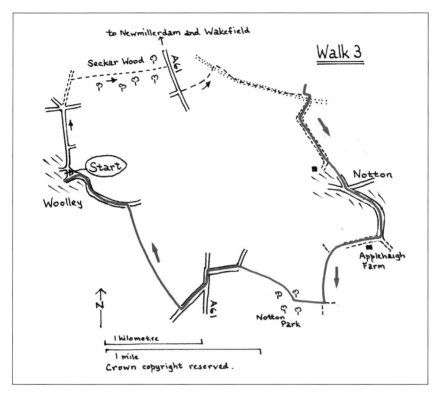

to Newmillerdam and Wakefield

Seckar Wood

Walk 3

Start

Woolley

Notton

Applehaigh Farm

Notton Park

N

1 kilometre

1 mile

Crown copyright reserved.

arriving from Newmillerdam. At the next fork keep right to cross the railway by the bridge. Your path is now a cart-track which is to be followed nearly all the way to Notton, first straight ahead parallel with the power lines, then sharp left by a single stone gatepost *(at this point there are extensive views of mainly open country all around),* right again by another solitary gatepost and almost as far as the gate of Manor Farm. But not quite. You will see in the hedgerow to your left a wooden footbridge over a beck, and then the path runs alongside the hedges and fences of houses until it finally emerges between houses into an estate road in Notton.

Turn right, then left at the junction into Ingswell Drive, then left again when you reach the main road through the village. After about 50 yards you reach The Green, a triangle of public open space. Turn right along its top edge (Applehaigh Lane) past the post office. Follow the lane through and out of the village. When you reach a fork go right and a few yards further on head straight on as the tarmac sweeps left to Applehaigh Farm. The track passes in front of cottages and farm buildings; as it swings left through a gate, you must go straight on over a stile and along a grass path to enter the attractive wooded area of Applehaigh Clough. Follow the path nearest the beck all the way through the clough, with the beck on the right, ignoring all potential diversions, including a footbridge over the beck.

On emerging from the trees, the path rises to reach a fence and stile visible at the top of a low bank. Once over the stile, continue ahead along a good broad track. When the track acquires trees on both sides, where the rooftops of Royston can be glimpsed to the left, a crossing path is reached. Turn right here and cross the field to enter the pleasant, mixed woodland of Notton Park. As soon as you enter the wood, keep right at the fork, then follow the central path until at another major fork you curve right and descend. On the way down a path comes in from the left and shortly before you leave the wood you pass a little pond a few yards to the left. Emerge from the wood and continue between fields, with a wooden fence on the left. When the fence ends, keep along the right hand edge of the field, soon on a track, which leads to a narrow tarmac road, Keeper Lane.

Cross over and turn left along the lane to the A61. Cross it and turn left up the footway. Turn right into the next minor road (Warren Lane). Look out for a pair of old stone gateposts into the wood on the right, which mark the start of a bridleway, go through and follow the path straight through the wood. Emerge at the other side through another pair of gateposts and keep forward with the wood on your right. When the wood ends, the bridleway should go straight across the field in front, which is at present planted with willow, but your only route across may be a tractor trail. On the far side keep forward, now on a clear track.

You can see on the hillside to your left the remains of a spoil heap that was once associated with the mine workings around the former Woolley Colliery and in the distance half right the rooftops of Wakefield. Ignore a track going off to the right alongside a cess pit and continue past the raised and fenced area on the left. The track becomes metalled as it passes a weighbridge and Mount Farm liquid fertiliser plant. On reaching New Road, cross and turn left along the footway to return to Woolley village. When you reach the green, the Wakefield Way bears left to continue up High Street. *[To continue with the route of the WW, jump to p.17]*

Walk 4
Woolley to Bretton Hall

Length of walk 8.54 miles (13.75 km), of which 5.44 miles (8.75 km) is Wakefield Way. Wide-ranging views. The walk includes Bretton Country Park and the Yorkshire Sculpture Park and the highest point of the Wakefield Way at 541 feet (165 metres). It starts and finishes at the village green in Woolley.

By bus: 58 Wakefield-Barnsley (Mon-Sat hourly).

By car: Park beside the village green in Woolley near the village hall.

With your back to the entrance into the village hall turn right and walk to the far corner of the green, **where the Wakefield Way comes in along New Road. Turn right, keeping the green on your right, and walk up High Street. At the top** (there is a bench and a charming little garden with the war memorial) **turn left along Church Street.** Restored in 1871, the church is built in the perpendicular style and dates mainly from the 15th and 16th centuries. It does however contain several relics of an earlier period. To gain admittance to the church, see the notice in the porch. **Immediately after passing the church go through a stile on the left into the churchyard and walk down past the church,** passing between two unusual tomb chests with pitched roofs of indeterminate age, **to a kissing-gate in the bottom wall, then straight down along the avenue of mature trees in the next field. Just before you reach the wall corner at the bottom turn right and walk across the large field, heading for the house on the far side. Cross the stile and bear left along the house drive to the road.**

　　Turn left for a short distance, then right along a minor road. At the far end of the second field on the right cross the stile by the gate on the right and walk up the right hand edge of the field to the stile a few yards to the left of the gate at the top. Cross and turn left along the bottom edge of the next field, in a short distance crossing a stile

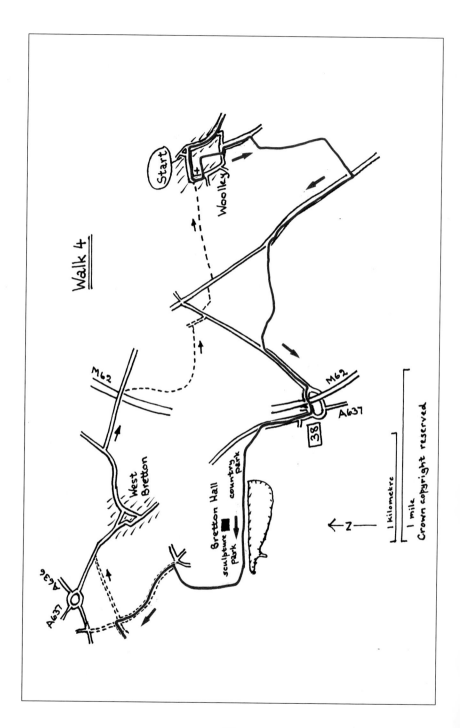

Walk 4

Start

Woolley

M62

M62

A637

38

West Bretton

Bretton Hall
sculpture park
country park

A637
A636

← N

1 kilometre
1 mile
Crown copyright reserved

by a gate. Keep forward towards the wood. After a time the path bears right away from the fence and makes for the top corner of the wood. *There is a magnificent prospect behind and to the left, including the Wakefield city skyline.* Cross the stile by the corner of Wheatley Wood and walk along with the wood on your left. *At 541 feet (165 metres) this is the highest point on the Wakefield Way.* At the end of the wood pass round the redundant stile ahead and turn right along the track. Follow the hedge on your right through this site of a former mine to reach Woolley Edge Lane.

Look left for a view of Barnsley, then turn right. There is a broad verge on the left hand side. A few yards after Gypsy Lane on the right and opposite the memorial to several victims of an accident in 1993, take the signposted path on the left which drops into the wood. Some way down look out for a not very clear fork and keep right. (If you miss it, you will come to a cross path: turn right along this to get back on track.) In a few yards you will meet the cross path coming in from the left. Bear left out of the wood and walk down the left hand edge of the field. At the bottom keep straight forward by the hedge on your left. Soon you are more clearly on a track. Follow this past Near Moor Farm on the right and on to a road (Haigh Lane). Cross and turn left. There is now no option but to cross the MI at its junction with the A637. So pass under the low railway bridge, over the River Dearne *(and briefly out of Wakefield District)* and under the motorway. Ignore the motorway access road and turn right along Huddersfield Road. Cross the road where convenient (perhaps near the bus lay-by) and continue along the footway, which leads onto the old road. At the end of this keep on along the footway. Before a lodge turn left through iron gates and walk along the tarmac drive, bearing right with this to reach the Bretton Country Park car-park, Information Centre, café *(open 10-4 at weekends and on school and bank holidays)* and toilets *(not always open).* As you approach the Information Centre you will see to the left a kissing-gate, which is your onward route.

Bretton Country Park and the Yorkshire Sculpture Park are worth an extended visit. In this glorious parkland, landscaped in the style of Capability Brown and now a Site of Scientific Interest, there are a lake, a woodland walk, a bird sanctuary, and an extensive and varied collection of sculpture, by Henry Moore and Barbara Hepworth among others, dotted about in the open air over several acres. In the magnificent new Visitor Centre there are toilets and refreshment areas (but open only until 6pm), a shop and various other exhibitions, and there are several galleries displaying modern art nearby. Bretton Hall, now part of Leeds

University, was built in the 1720s as a home for Sir William Wentworth.

From the kissing gate keep forward along the broad path, in a few yards bearing right where another track comes in from the left. A few yards further on keep straight on for the Sculpture Park Visitor Centre, but the Wakefield Way forks left, soon passing two of the Moore sculptures. *Just down here is a charming 18th-century bridge over the end of the lake, to which you might like to make a brief diversion.* Our route however continues straight ahead with the lake to our left. Pass through two gates. *(Waymarks indicate that you are on both the Barnsley Boundary Walk and the Dearne Way, as well as the Wakefield Way.)* The footpath then passes between low trees, emerging just below the Hall.

Keep straight ahead, following the line of the water channel. Just before you reach a sculpture formed out of breeze blocks, one of the park's permanent pieces entitled "123454321", you need to head slightly right to a track, along which you bear left to a kissing-gate with a broad track beyond. Turn right, through another gate, and walk alongside an iron fence on the right. Shortly after a track forks off left signposted to Clayton West, another track goes off right into the Sculpture Park and you reach a fork: keep left here, soon passing through a metal gate, after which the track is heading for a house. The track passes through another gate and to the right of the house. Where the track bends right to join a tarmac road at a junction, go through the large wooden gate on the left and follow the track up through the parkland.

From the highest point admire the panorama, from Barnsley to the left round by High Hoyland and Clayton West to the Holme Moss mast and the Pennines in the distance, with Emley and its mast closer to you. Pass through an iron gate out of the park into the wood. In a few yards a path joins you from the right and soon you reach a crossing of tracks. The Wakefield Way turns left here, *[To continue with the route of the WW, jump to p.22]* but you turn right. Follow this track to the A637, cross and turn right. Enter West Bretton and take the first road forking left (signposted Village Hall & Church). *At the end of the village you pass Bretton Post Office and become aware of the M1 again over on the right. The Wakefield skyline is visible to the left.* Take the first road on the right (Bramley Lane). It leads across the motorway. *Immediately before the bridge there is access to Woolley Edge Motorway Services on the left.*

Immediately after the bridge turn right along the signposted Walkway, bearing left on an indistinct path which leads along the edge of the wood. *You are walking on top of a railway tunnel, hence the airshafts you pass, and many of the unevennesses in the terrain must be old spoil heaps from the tunnel.* Drop down a little, to leave the elevated path by some steps on the right, then left down some more. Bear left at the bottom. The path through the wood is reasonably clear, but can be very overgrown. Eventually it bears left down some more steps, crosses a footbridge and emerges into a field. Bear left along the bottom edge of the field, and when you reach the boundary wall of Savin Royd Wood, turn right and walk up the edge of the field with the wood on your left.

Cross a stile and continue up beside the wood. At the top edge of the wood cross the stile and turn right along the track to the road. Turn left for 80 yards to a signposted footpath on the right. Cross the stile and walk straight across the field to a fence corner, then on with the fence to your left to a stile in the next corner. Cross and turn left up an enclosed path. When the wall on the right ends at an old gatepost, bear left to a stile in the fence ahead and climb some steps to return to Woolley Edge Lane. Turn right for 40 yards to a signposted path on the left. It leads along the left hand edge of the field. *There is an extensive prospect ahead, and soon the tower of Woolley Church comes back into view.* Where the fence ends and a hedge starts, cross the stile and continue with the hedge on your right.

Go through a small gate beside a large one and walk down the track into Woolley. Walk straight forward down High Street to return to the green.

archaeological remains in Woolley - but what are they?

Walk 5
Bank Wood and Stony Cliffe Wood

Walk length 5.28 miles (8.5 km), of which 3.1 miles (5 km) is Wakefield Way. A most attractive mix of old tracks and woodland paths in undulating countryside with good views, two nature reserves and much of historical interest.

By bus: *231 Wakefield-Huddersfield (Mon-Sat hourly), 447/448 Wakefield-Denby Dale (Mon.-Sat. hourly, Sun. 2-hourly), 935 Wakefield-Denby Dale-Holmfirth (hourly) to the roundabout at the junction of the A636 Wakefield-Denby Dale road and the A637 Barnsley-Grange Moor link road. Walk along towards Denby Dale for 300 yards to a car-park on the left. The walk starts here.*

By car: *On the A636 Wakefield-Denby Dale road, 300 yards on the Denby Dale side of the roundabout at the junction with the A637 on Bretton Common, opposite a minor road on the right there is a car park on the left. Park here. If it is full, there are laybys along the minor road.*

Walk to the far end of the car park, cross the stile by the gate and take the track through the woods. Shortly after passing a viewing platform on the right turn right at a cross track, **here joining the Wakefield Way, and follow it down through the wood. Leave the wood by a gate and pass a track leading to Bower Hill Farm on the right. Keep down the tree-lined path to the A636, cross and take the Emley road opposite. Turn right along the access road to Bentley Grange,** *but before you do, look*

stepping stones over Bank Wood Beck

left to the grassy hillock which is the remains of bell pits, where monks of Byland Abbey who owned Bentley Grange used to mine iron.
   At the farm, where the track forks, keep right, and at the entrance into the farmyard go through the gate on the right

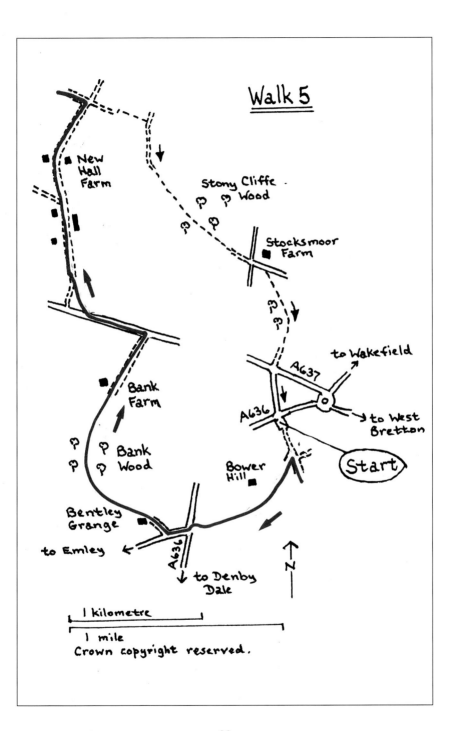

Walk 5

New Hall Farm

Stony Cliffe Wood

Stocksmoor Farm

to Wakefield

A637

A636

to West Bretton

Start

Bank Farm

Bank Wood

Bower Hill

Bentley Grange

to Emley

A636

to Denby Dale

N

1 kilometre

1 mile

Crown copyright reserved.

and walk along the track to the right of the buildings. At the end of all the buildings bear right with the track and continue with a high hedge on your left. *We have now briefly left Wakefield District for Kirklees.* At the end of the fruit bushes go through the gate ahead and continue by the hedge. On reaching a wide fenced gap in the hedge bear half right down the field to a stile on the edge of the wood. Cross this and the footbridge beyond over Little Dyke and walk along with Bank Wood Beck on your right until you reach stepping stones over it. Cross these *(we're now back in Wakefield District)* and the stile ahead into Bank Wood and bear left up through it.

The path soon bears left parallel to the beck down below, but look out for a sleeper bridge on the right followed by a flight of steps climbing through the wood. In summer the path through Bank Wood can be very overgrown. Where the ground levels out, cross over a grassy ride and keep on up the narrow path. *You are on Furnace Hill, where charcoal was burnt and iron smelted in the 14th century.* Further up you reach a grassy, rather indistinct cross track: turn left along this, but after 80 yards fork right off it on a footpath up some more steps. Cross the stile out of the wood and keep forward to the right of a hedge.

At Bank Farm walk along the right hand edge of the farmyard, and follow the access road up to the A637. Cross to the footway and turn left. Shortly before the water tower a footpath sign points right over a stile. Bear slightly left over the field to a stile in the bottom corner *(fine views right).* Turn left through the gap by the gate then right down the tarmac access road to New Hall Detention Centre. When you reach a fork keep right and follow the road straight through between the houses, but where just after the telephone kiosk it turns left, keep straight on up a narrow lane.

Follow the track through New Hall Farm, *noticing the remains of the mediaeval moat and the carved head on the building on the right which came from a 13th-century chapel which once stood near here.* On reaching a junction of tracks, the Wakefield Way turns left and heads for the telecommunications masts, *[To continue with the route of the WW, jump to p.27]* but we keep straight on, in a few yards bearing right at the fork. After passing a house, the old road narrows to a footpath, at first hedged, then following the left hand edge of a field. When you reach a cross path, turn right down it. Follow it all the way down, to pass between two substantial stone gateposts, cross a wooden bridge and enter the nature reserve of Stony Cliffe Wood.

Continue on the broad rising track with a fence on the left. The path leads up through the wood, leaves it, and a short stretch of narrow

at New Hall Farm

hedged path leads to a tarmac road. Bear left up this, and at the crossroads go straight over and along the narrow road opposite. After 150 yards, having passed Stocksmoor Farm on the left, fork right off the road by a signpost which says Stocksmoor Common. Follow the main path through the wood. After a time a path comes in from the left and there is a fork ahead: keep left and soon you are close to the left hand edge of the wood. Cross a stile by a gate and the path becomes a track which leads to the A637. Cross over and follow the minor road opposite. Cross the A636 to reach the car park and the start of the walk.

Walk 6
Horbury Bridge, Netherton, Overton, Emroyd Common and Middlestown

Walk length 8.23 miles (13.25 km), of which 5 miles (8 km) is Wakefield Way). A lovely walk, almost entirely rural, often idyllic, with many fine views. Slightly strenuous, as there are many ups and downs. A visit to the National Coal Mining Museum of England, the attractions of which include a café, can be included halfway round. The walk starts at Horbury Bridge.

By bus: 128/129 Wakefield-Dewsbury (every 20/40 mins), 231/232 Wakefield-Huddersfield (hourly), 265 Wakefield-Netherton (hourly) to Horbury Bridge.

By car: You will probably find room to park at Horbury Bridge on Bridge Road opposite the school or in nearby St. John's Street.

Walk down to the right of the Bingley Arms onto the towpath of the Calder & Hebble Navigation *(which links the Aire & Calder Navigation at Wakefield to Sowerby Bridge and Manchester. Evidence of coal mining in the countryside around Horbury points to one of the reasons for the Navigation's construction)* and walk forward along it. Pass under the first bridge, but cross the canal by the second, rusty metal one and walk up the track. *The first of the walk's extensive views opens up behind you as you climb, with the spires of Horbury and Ossett churches prominent.* Pass Netherton Cricket Club, and when you reach the road in Netherton, cross it and turn left. Ignore the first public footpath sign immediately, but at the end of the next short terrace of houses turn right up a signposted track. Where the garden fence on the left turns left, go with it along an enclosed path behind the houses which leads to a stile.

Walk down the right hand edge of the field, passing a large metal gate, until you come to a stile on the right. Cross it and bear left down the left hand edge of the next field, soon turning left out of the field and dropping to cross Pits Beck by a footbridge. Climb the other side to a stile into the next field and walk straight up, aiming well to the right of the wood ahead. *Again there is a splendid view back, extending this time to the Wakefield city skyline.* Cross a stile onto a hedged path and turn right, in a few yards crossing another stile. Pass a brick house, and now you are on a track. When the track bends left, keep straight on over a stile by a gate, and follow the hedge on your left. At the end of the field cross a stile and keep forward along the tarmac drive. Follow it to a road and turn right to Upper Lane,

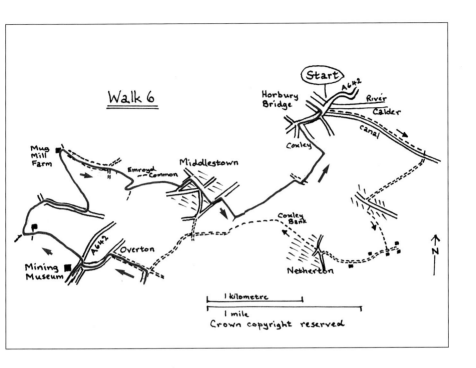

Walk 6

Netherton. *The Star Inn is on the right, Netherton post office on the left.*

Cross straight over into the track opposite, pass round the end of the fence ahead and keep straight on on a tarmac path. Cross straight over the next road into the grassy track opposite. *Netherton Village Hall is to the left, and there are more superb views.* Walk down the right hand edge of the next field and at the bottom go down the steps into the wood. *You are now on Coxley Bank, with the Coxley Valley ahead.* Walk down the broad steps, crossing over a cross track. Near the bottom of the wood cross over another cross path and bear left, with ponds to the right, soon forking right to cross the beck by a footbridge and walk up the field with the fence on your right.

At the top cross the stile by the gate and bear left along the track behind the houses. On reaching the next houses, on the southern edge of Middlestown, turn right at the T-junction (Carr Lane), but in a few yards go left along a track (Chapel Hill Lane). After a time the track climbs quite steeply. Near the top a path goes off to the right and a track comes in from the left and at the top we reach a junction. **The Wakefield Way comes in along the track ahead and to the left, so we join it here by turning right along the track towards the telecommunications masts.** *Again there are extensive views.* **When you reach the road in Overton, cross**

and turn left along the footway. Some way along fork right onto a narrow lane which leads down to the A642. Cross the main road. If you want to visit the Mining Museum turn left, then return to this point, otherwise turn right. *The museum offers excellent displays, an underground tour of a former mine, a café and toilets. The mine (Caphouse Colliery) closed in 1987.*

A short distance along the A642 take the footpath signposted down some steps on the left. It leads down the edge of a wood. Cross a stile into a field and turn left down its edge to cross another stile and a bridge over the beck. *Here we pass briefly into Kirklees District.* Bear right along the right hand edge of the field with the beck on your right. Cross the stile in the corner and keep along the edge of the next field, soon bearing left with the hedge. Cross a track leading to Haslegreave Farm on the right by two stiles and continue along the right hand edge of the next field. Cross the stile in the next corner and turn right along the track, but when this bears right to the farm, keep straight forward along another track with a hedge on the left. It leads to a road (Wood Lane) *where we re-enter Wakefield District.*

Keep forward up the road. Ignore the first public footpath sign on the left, but follow the second one, which is beside a large metal gate and has another signposted path on the other side of the road. Walk along close to the right hand edge of the field. The next stile leads into a lovely old path, Briggs Lane, still largely paved. Follow it down until just before Mug Mill Farm a track comes in from the right. Turn along this. At a fork ignore both tracks, cross the stile straight ahead between them and walk straight through the trees to the stile on the far side. We shall now climb over Emroyd Common to Middlestown. Cross the stile and keep straight up the hill to the next one, then half right over the next field to the next one and half left over the next field to the one after that. Turn right up the stepped path along the edge of the wood.

At the top turn left along a broad cross path. At a fork keep right along the narrower path, and at the next fork again keep right on the narrower path, now with garden fences on the right and soon on both sides. The path leads out to a street in Middlestown. Turn left. At the T-junction turn right along the footway to the A642. Cross it by the pedestrian crossing and bear slightly left to take the narrow ascending tarmac path to the right of the White Swan. When the tarmac ends, follow the path up the right hand edge of a field, then on to the next road. Turn left for about 60 yards, then take the hedged path on the right. On reaching a field, keep along its right hand edge.

At the far end of the field bear right out of it, walk down some steps, keep left at the fork and left again in a few yards at the next fork on a path which contours high in the wood. Keep on this high path, not far from the top edge of the wood, all the way to a broad cross path. Turn left here, with the fence on your right, and follow this path to Coxley. When you reach a tarmac lane, turn right down it. At the bottom, when you reach a large open space, turn left at the start of this along a track, which leads down the Coxley Valley. At times the beck is close by on your left. Keeping always to the main path down the valley, eventually you bear left on a paved path by the side of the beck.

Pass through a barrier and keep forward up the road (Water Lane Close). At the top keep straight forward, at the T-junction turn right to the A642 and follow it back to Horbury Bridge. The Wakefield Way continues along the lane on the left between the canal bridge and the river bridge. *[To continue with the route of the WW, jump to p.30]*

Newmillerdam
(page 13)

Walk 7
Horbury Bridge to Chickenley

Walk length 6.37 miles (10.25 km) of which 3.26 miles (5.25 km) is Wakefield Way. Field paths, disused railways, an attractive stretch of canal towpath and fine views of the Calder valley. The walk includes 3 km of the Kirklees Way.

By bus: 128/129 Wakefield-Dewsbury (every 20/40 mins), 231/232 Wakefield-Huddersfield (hourly), 265 Wakefield-Netherton (hourly) to Horbury Bridge.

By car: You will probably find room to park at Horbury Bridge on Bridge Road opposite the school or in nearby St. John's Street.

Between the river and canal bridges turn into the lane on the opposite side of the road to the Bingley Arms. When the surface ends keep on along the track, and just before this enters a field look right for a view of a delightful little marina, then go left onto the towpath of the Calder & Hebble Navigation and turn right along it. There follows an attractive stretch of peaceful rural canal. After about a mile pass two locks, a house and a small bridge over a cut on the right and immediately fork right (here joining the Kirklees Way) **on a path which leads through a tunnel under the railway. Now you have the Calder close by on the right. Pass through another tunnel under railway lines and then under a substantial railway bridge and keep forward by the river, which you soon cross by a footbridge.**

Walk on to reach a tarmac road and turn left along it, to pass through a gap-stile by a large metal gate and enter the grounds of a factory. Walk along the right hand edge of these and keep on up the lane with a high wall on your right. Ignore a path forking right to a stile by a large gate and keep on along the right hand edge of the factory yard, then the track outside the car park, to a stile by a double metal gate. Keep forward along the track over the field, parallel to the fence on your right. On entering the next field, fork left to find a clear but narrow path a little below the level of the field, with trees on the left and soon with a fence on the right. When you reach the high fence of the Dewsbury Waste Water Treatment Works, keep to the right of it, into the field, and in a few yards turn right uphill with an old wall on your left. Follow the path, which bears slightly right away from the wall, into the next field, turn left for a yard or two to the corner, then right, to follow once again the old wall.

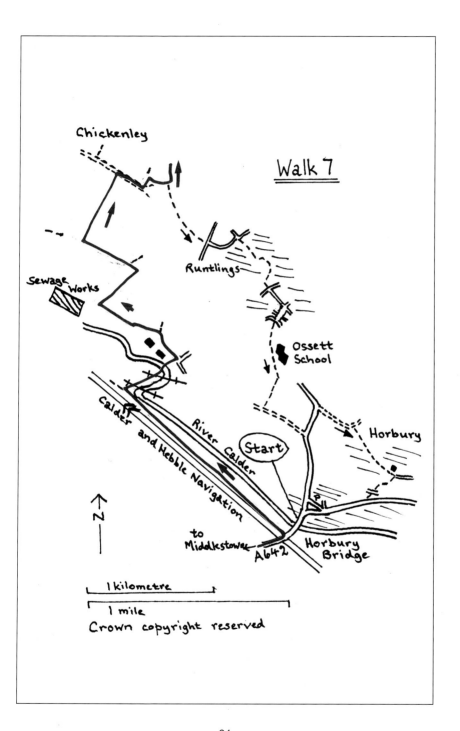

Chickenley

Walk 7

Runtlings

Sewage Works

Ossett School

Horbury

Start

River Calder

Calder and Hebble Navigation

N

to Middlestown

A642

Horbury Bridge

1 kilometre

1 mile

When the wall turns sharp left at a redundant stile, turn left and walk along with the wall now on your right, in 10 yards turning right again with the wall and continuing up with the wall still on your right. There is at present no path. (There may be a clear path on the other side of the wall, but this is not the right of way.) When you reach a broad path coming up from your left, turn sharp left down it. *On the other side of the valley on the hill is Thornhill.*

In the bottom of the dip ignore a path coming in from the right (after rain you may have to jump Pildacre Mill Beck), and as you climb again there is young woodland on both sides. Just after crossing the brow of the hill take a track forking right, ignoring the track straight ahead, but just before the track bends left to cross a beck (there is an old stone gatepost here), keep straight forward up the left hand edge of the field with the beck down on your left. Keep the beck, *which is also the boundary between Wakefield and Kirklees Districts,* on your left until you are faced by a fence. Turn right, but when you reach a gap in the fence go through it and in a few yards turn right, *here leaving the Kirklees Way,* along the line of a former railway between hedges.

Where the path bends left and begins to climb, take the left hand, narrower path at a fork, keeping the small wood on your right, but shortly after the gradient eases turn right through a narrow gap in the fence onto a tarmac path and follow this across the park. *There are fine views over the Calder valley.* The path bends left and passes through another narrow gap in the fence. The Wakefield Way turns left here along the tarmac cross path, another former railway line, *[To continue with the route of the WW, jump to p.37]* but we turn right. When the tarmac ends, keep on along the grit path, eventually passing to the right of houses (ignore a path forking left up to them) until you reach the road in Runtlings through a kissing-gate. Turn left for a few yards, then take the first road on the right. *Notice the worn old paving stones a cartwheel's width apart.*

Now we wind our way through South Ossett, and close attention must be paid to route-finding! At the next junction turn right down the footway with a high hedge/fence on the left (ignoring the track on the right), pass the barrier and walk forward down Ash Close, turning left at the bottom to follow another tarmac path. At the T-junction turn right, but just before the entrance to Ossett Cricket Club turn left along an enclosed path. Follow it to the end, keep forward along the street and at the next junction bear right along Dimple Wells Lane. Follow it to the very end and turn left along a ginnel. Cross the next road diagonally left to walk along Broomcroft Road opposite. Turn right down Valley View Road and at the T-junction at the bottom turn left along Healey Drive. After house no. 40 on the right go down the ginnel, which soon turns left and then right again. Now our tour of the houses is over!

At the end ignore a fenced path on the right, cross the stile and keep forward along the left hand edge of the field to pass Ossett School. *Again there is a fine view up Calderdale.* At the end of the field turn right with the fence downhill. *There is a great array of railway sidings ahead.* Follow the fence down to a cross track, turn left along it and follow it to the road. By turning right you could return quickly to Horbury Bridge, but there are more delights in store! So turn left uphill. Where the road curves left there is a large layby on the right.

Take the signposted bridleway leaving the layby. Where the track bends left uphill, fork right off it along a tarmac path. Pass a metal barrier. This pleasant path leads through between gardens. At the end go down some steps on the right and turn left. The tarmac surface resumes and there is a fine Georgian house on the left. Opposite it take the hedged ginnel on the right and follow it all the way down to a cross street. Cross and walk up the path to the main road. Turn right to return to Horbury Bridge.

grooves caused by towropes on Barnsley Canal (see page 8)

Walk 8
Gawthorpe, Chidswell, Hanging Heaton and Earlsheaton

Walk length 6.37 miles (10.25 km), of which 1.71 miles (2.75 km) is Wakefield Way. It proved impossible to design a satisfactory circular walk in this area in the Wakefield District, which explains the short distance of Wakefield Way covered on this walk. Much of it is in neighbouring Kirklees, including a section of Kirklees Way and the spectacular high contouring path along Cracken Edge. A circuit of considerable interest and superb views. The walk starts at the maypole in Gawthorpe. Gawthorpe possesses one of the few permanently located maypoles (the first erected in 1850), where Mayday celebrations are held on the first Saturday in May. The village also hosts every Easter a fiercely contested coal-carrying competition.

By bus: 116/117 Wakefield-Dewsbury/Leeds (half-hourly) to Gawthorpe High Street. Continue along the High Street to the maypole.

By car: There is signposted car-parking in the centre of Gawthorpe near the maypole on Cross Street opposite the Gawthorpe Surgery.

With your back to the maypole and facing along the main road through Gawthorpe, turn left along School Street (signposted public footpath). At the end of the street cross the stile and walk straight forward up the field (if the field has a growing crop, a tractor track should mark the footpath). The path proceeds straight across this very large field until just past the highest point, where it bears left to the top corner, but the tractor track will probably take you straight across to the far side, where another one will take you left up to the corner. Cross the stile, footbridge, stile in the corner and bear left to a stile by the gate just to the left of the buildings. Cross the stile and bear right to a small gate into the car-park of the Huntsman Inn, then turn left to the road.

Cross the road and turn right along the footway. At the next junction keep straight ahead and follow the road as far as Chidswell Lane on the left. Turn along here and follow the footway to the A653. Cross straight over and walk down a short unmade road opposite towards a high green fence. Take the path to the right of the fence, but where the fence turns left, keep straight on past an old stone gatepost and through some trees to pick up a tarmac path with football pitches to the right. When the tarmac ends, climb the bank on the left to a stile, cross it and walk along

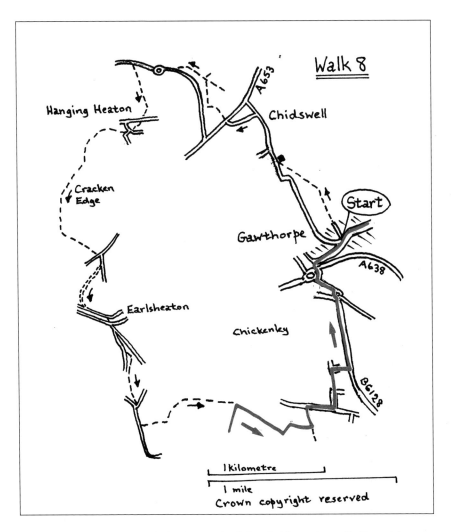

Walk 8

Hanging Heaton

Chidswell

Cracken Edge

Start

Gawthorpe

A638

Earlsheaton

Chickenley

B6128

1 Kilometre

1 mile

Crown copyright reserved

the top edge of the field. At the end of the field go through the wide gap in the hedge, and a clear path bears right over the next field to the hedge/fence on the far side, then makes its way down the field close to the left hand edge, becoming a track which leads out through a gate (with a stile beside it).

Ignoring the track straight ahead, turn left down a cross track, an old road (Grange Road). When you reach the B6128 at metal bollards, turn right along the footway. At the roundabout keep straight on *(notice the two old stone gateposts in the middle of it),* crossing the road where convenient. After the second house on the right you will notice a footpath coming down from the right. Turn left here along a path between high metal fences *(a blue K indicates that here we join the Kirklees Way)*. Our route now takes us up the hill to Hanging Heaton. The path is fenced almost all the way. Steps lead through a stile, and more steps lead on up to houses. Walk up the concrete drive to a road, cross and turn right for a few yards to a short flight of steps on the left. Up these turn right, but just after the telephone kiosk fork left up another flight of steps. Turn right at the next street, cross the end of a road coming up from the right and fork right along a tarmac path signposted "10A and 10B Kirkgate".

When the tarmac ends, keep forward along the track, which soon narrows to a footpath. The view to the right is over Batley. *There now follows a splendid high contouring path with ever-changing and wide-ranging views. Castle Hill above Huddersfield and West Nab beyond, then the Emley Moor mast come into view.* Follow this path until you reach a stile with a notice "Dangerous Footpath: No Public Access". Here you must turn right, steeply down the slope, to join a lower path, where you turn left over a stile. A short distance along ignore a flight of steps on the right. The path passes below a much-graffitied escarpment, then bends right, descending gently to a broad cross path. Turn left. Pass a modern pyramidal sculpture and bear left past a barrier to walk along a short street to the busy A653.

tree sculpture in Haw Park (page 7)

Cross and bear right up Sugar Lane. A short way up fork right down a track which soon becomes grassy. Cross over a cross path. On reaching houses the track broadens to an unmade road. Ignoring a road on the right, keep on down to a T-junction and turn left *(here leaving the Kirklees Way)*. As you climb, look out for four bollards on the right: pass through and follow the old cobbled track to another four bollards at the far end and the A638. Cross the main road (care!) and take the minor road diagonally left opposite, in a few yards forking right down Middle Road. Twenty yards after the end of the houses on the left fork left onto a signposted climbing footpath. Ignore the road at the top and keep forward down another cobbled path, soon forking left off the cobbles along a contouring grassy path.

After a time the path passes below some houses. Climb a few steps on the left to a road and turn right down the road to a broad junction. Cross straight over into Headland Lane opposite, which in a few yards seems to become Long Lane. Pass South Terrace on the left, and a short distance further along turn left down a track *(now you are back on the Kirklees Way)*. Cross the stile at the end and walk down the right hand edge of the field to another stile at the bottom. Cross the beck by the footbridge and turn left with a fence on the right. When the fence ends, keep on up the track. About 40 yards before the track reaches a metal barrier fork right uphill, leaving the houses to your left.

Opposite a track on the left you are joined by a path from the field on the right. *Here we leave the Kirklees Way for the last time, re-enter Wakefield District* **and join the Wakefield Way. The path starts to climb and you reach a fork. Keep left on the narrower path, soon with a fence on the right. Shortly after the gradient eases go through a narrow gap in the fence and follow a tarmac path across the park.** *The views over the Calder valley are magnificent.* **The path curves left and passes through a gap in another fence to reach a cross path. Turn left along this former railway track. When you reach a car-park, walk along its right hand edge and climb the steps to a road.**

Cross the road and turn right up the footway. At the top of the hill turn left (Love Lane) and walk along the front of a terrace of stone-built houses, then continue forward along the footway. When the main street turns right, take the left fork along a short stretch of tarmac road, which leads into a hedged footpath. When this ends, keep forward for a few yards, then take the first street on the right (Holmfield). At the end keep forward along a ginnel which leads to the B6128. Turn left along the footway and follow it all the way to a major roundabout.

Walk clockwise round the roundabout and take the second exit. Cross this road when convenient and cross the A638 by the footbridge. Having descended the steps at the other side go straight ahead into Gawthorpe, passing a primary school to your left, and soon you will return to the maypole. *[To continue with the route of the WW, jump to p.38]*

Walk 9
Gawthorpe to Kirkhamgate

Walk length 5.6 miles (9 km), of which 2.17 miles (3.5 km) is Wakefield Way. A long, easy stretch on an old track (Gawthorpe Lane) is followed by the short climb to Lindale Hill, a fine viewpoint for Wakefield and beyond. The return includes a pleasant stretch by Alverthorpe Beck, a short piece of road and field paths with more extensive views. The walk starts at the maypole in Gawthorpe.

By bus: 116/117 Wakefield-Dewsbury/Leeds (half-hourly) to Gawthorpe High Street. Continue along the High Street to the maypole.

By car: There is signposted car-parking in the centre of Gawthorpe near the maypole on Cross Street opposite the Gawthorpe Surgery.

From the maypole follow the main street through Gawthorpe, soon signposted as a no through road. Pass the Beehive Inn on the right and further along Highfield School on the left. Beyond the school follow the tarmac lane. Some way down, immediately after the junction with another tarmac lane on the left, the tarmac surface ends. Further on ignore a track to the left to Lower Park Farm. Just after Park Grange Farm keep right at the fork. *The M1 is now visible ahead. At its lowest point the track crosses Bushy Beck Bridge,* **then starts its ascent, passing under the motorway and climbing to the main road in Kirkhamgate.**

Cross the road and turn right along the footway. Pass Lindhill Nurseries on the left, and a short distance further along, opposite Lindale Farm on the right, turn left up a track. Where the track bends left to a house, keep forward past the gate and up a path in a broad hedged way. By a power line pole the path splits into three: take the middle, broadest path up onto Lindale Hill, *which soon affords an extensive view right. The sturdy square tower is Alverthorpe Church, which we shall pass later in the walk, with further off the Wakefield city skyline.* **Continue down the broad grassy path, which soon narrows and leads down by a hedge on the right to a cross track (Lindale Lane). The Wakefield Way turns left here,** *[To continue with the route of the WW, jump to p.44]* **but our way is to the right.**

Just before you reach the houses there is at present a field of rhubarb on the right. *The area bounded by Wakefield, Dewsbury and Leeds is the "Rhubarb Triangle", where rhubarb has been intensively cultivated since the 1870s. After a long period of decline the industry is enjoying*

Walk 9

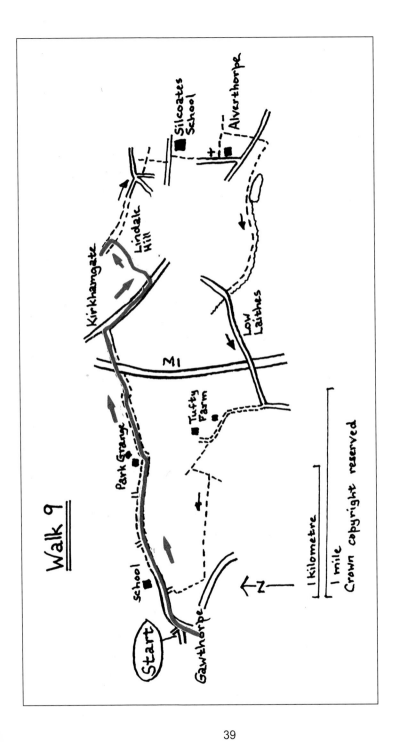

Kirkhamgate

Lindale Hill

Silcoates School

Alverthorpe

M1

Low Laithes

Park Grange

Tuffy Farm

school

Start

Gawthorpe

←N—

1 Kilometre

1 mile

something of a resurgence (West Yorkshire produces 90% of Britain's rhubarb crop) and Wakefield MDC now offers gastronomic tours and an annual rhubarb festival. For details contact the Tourist Information Centre. The track becomes a street with houses on both sides. At the next junction cross straight over the main road into Sunnyhill Crescent, but in 30 yards turn left along a tarmac drive which leads to a large grassy area. Walk along the right hand edge of this and at the end turn right along a paved path, ignoring another paved path forking left almost immediately.

Hill Top Road, Newmillerdam (page 13)

Follow the path to where it ends at a barrier and a street. Cross the street and turn left. Ignore The Mount on the right, but 30 yards further on turn right along Toll Bar Lane. Pass Silcoates School on the left. *The school was founded in 1809 and re-founded in 1820. The main school buildings were built after a fire in 1904.* The track narrows. Join a road and keep forward to pass to the right of St. Paul's Church, Alverthorpe, *which dates from 1823-25.* At the end of the church grounds turn left, pass through a barrier and along a path with the church on the left and a school down on the right. The path widens out into a grassy area. Halfway along this turn right down a tarmac path leading past a barrier into a housing estate. Walk straight down, at the junction at the foot bear right for a few yards to find the continuing path on the left which leads down to a yard. Walk straight forward across the yard, down a few steps at the far side and out onto the main road.

Cross and turn left, but immediately after Alverthorpe Garage turn right along a path which leads along a grassy area to a cross street (Green Lane). Cross straight over and take the dirt track opposite, which soon curves right. Where the track ends, the path forks: keep left along the unsurfaced path, which soon becomes an attractive hedged avenue. Through the hedge on the left an old mill pond can be seen, popular with anglers. At what looks like the end of the avenue, keep on along the clear path, still with the pond on the left, and soon you drop to a path junction: cross the cross path and bear left and you find yourself back in the hedged avenue. Where it ends again, pass under power lines and keep forward on a narrow path with a hedge on the right.

When faced by a gate, turn sharp left with a fence on the right. In a few yards you reach a junction with Alverthorpe Beck ahead. Turn right here, still with a fence on the right, and Low Laithes golf course on the other side of the beck. For quite a distance now the path stays fairly close to the beck, then turns into a track which leads to a road. Turn left, cross the bridge over Alverthorpe Beck and follow the road past the entrance to Low Laithes Golf Club and over the motorway. At the top of the hill, where the road turns sharp left, take the track on the right to Tufty Farm. *There are good views from this track back towards Wakefield.* Pass a detached brick house. When the track bends right to descend to the farm, cross a stile in the fence on the left and bear right along the right hand edge of the field.

Where you pass under three power lines coming down the hill, turn left and follow these lines up the slope to reach a track. Don't turn right to follow the track along with the hedge on the left, but turn right just beyond the hedge and follow it along on your right, all the way to the houses of Gawthorpe. Cross the stile and turn right along the tarmac path. When you reach a junction with four steps on the left, bear right between fences. Turn left along the next street. When you reach the main road through Gawthorpe, turn left to return to the maypole.

Rose Farm (page 12)

41

Walk 10
Kirkhamgate and Carr Gate
to Outwood Station

Walk length 6.21 miles (10 km), of which 3.26 miles (5.25 km) is Wakefield Way.

By train: From Wakefield and Leeds to Outwood Station

By car: Park at Outwood Station. For the main car-park drive down Lingwell Court on the Leeds side of the road bridge over the railway, but for a smaller, quieter car-park, turn down Railway Terrace at the Wakefield end of the bridge and follow it to its end.

Leave Outwood Station *("Outwood" means simply "the wood outside" Wakefield)* and turn right along the road, crossing it where convenient. Turn left along the first track (Grandstand Road -. *horse races were held here during the second half of the 18th century; although no trace remains of the 2-mile course, it is thought to have been bounded by Lawns Lane and Grandstand Road),* but at the end of the houses and gardens on the left turn left along a footpath, soon with a grassy bank on the right. After a time the broad, bordered path narrows and you are soon walking parallel to the railway, which you may hear but cannot see. Climb a few steps and keep forward along the tarmac path, with an industrial building on the right. When you reach a road, turn right along the footway. Cross the bridge over the A650 and about 100 yards further turn right along a tarmac footpath. Where the footway ends at the entrance to a car-park on the right, cross diagonally left and continue along the footway in the same direction as before.

A few yards before the roundabout on the A650 turn left along a short stretch of tarmac road, but at the end of the footway turn sharp left uphill on a tarmac path. When the tarmac ends, keep on by the fence/hedge on the right. Join the access drive to a bungalow and follow it down to the next road. Cross and turn left, but immediately before the first house on the right turn right down a tarmac drive, then keep straight on along the subsequent footpath. Turn left into the housing estate and right along the first street. At the T-junction at the end of the houses turn left, and immediately before the houses begin again on the right turn right along a signposted path between garden fences on the left and fields on the right. Part way along the path kinks left into a hedged/fenced path. This soon descends to cross a beck by a footbridge. Keep on the path to the next road. Cross it and turn right for a few yards, then take a tarmac path on the left between a school on the left and fields on the right. It crosses a beck by a footbridge and climbs to a street. Cross straight over and continue climbing. Cross the next road diagonally right to the continuation of the footpath. When you reach a large grassy area, turn right along its right hand edge. At the far end a tarmac track leads to a road. Cross this and turn right, then at the next junction cross straight over the road into Lindale Lane.

Soon the tarmac ends and you are on a broad stony track. Pass under power lines and pass a gate into a yard on the left. A few yards beyond

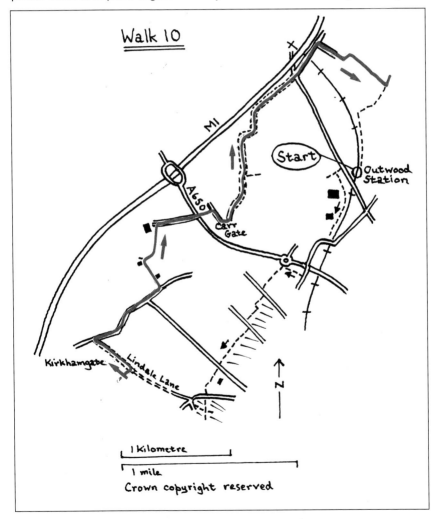

43

this a footpath comes in from the left down from Lindale Hill **and here you join the Wakefield Way. Eventually the track passes between houses and acquires a tarmac surface. Follow this street to where it ends at a T-junction and turn right along the footway. The footway on the other side is continuous, so cross to it where convenient. Almost at the top of the hill, and after the junction with Jerry Clay Lane, you reach the tarmac access drive to Aspen Farm on the left (signposted as a public footpath to East Ardsley). Turn along it. Immediately before the entrance gates into Aspen Farm go through the stile by the large gate on the left and walk down the track.**

Pass to the right of a cottage, now on grass. Go through a kissing-gate at the bottom and in three yards, where the path forks, keep right across scrubby woodland. After a time you have the fence of the Police Dog Training Establishment on the left. Go through a kissing-gate and turn right up the access road to this Establishment, on which there may well be much coming and going of police cars. Cross straight over the dual carriageway A650 (this may take some time!) and pass through the bollards into the footpath opposite. When you reach the next road, cross it and turn right. *A short distance along on the right is the Malt Shovel pub.* **Directly opposite the pub turn left up a tarmac access road, which narrows to a footpath and leads to another road (Lawns Lane).**

Turn left. The road narrows and soon becomes an unsurfaced track. After a time the M1 is close by on the left. Follow Lawns Lane to where it ends at a road. Turn left for a few yards, with the M1 bridge straight ahead, then turn right along Castle Head Lane. Cross the bridge over the railway and take the next minor road on the right (Lingwell Nook Lane). Pass the houses and keep forward up the track to a gate, ignoring a track forking right through another gate on the way. Pass round the gate, ignore a stile by another gate on the right in a few yards, and take the track which bends left. *You are now in what used to be Lofthouse Colliery.*

Follow this path until you reach a crossing: down the slope on the right comes a broad track, to cross a sleeper bridge just to your right, and on the left a footpath forks sharply back to cross a footbridge in a short distance. That is the onward route of the Wakefield Way, *[To continue with the route of the WW, jump to p.45]* but our walk takes the track on the right up the slope. Cross the flat top of the hill and follow the path down the other side. Cross the broad sleeper bridge and bear left along the track, with the railway fence on your right. Follow this fence back to Outwood Station, choosing always the path which stays closest to it.

Walk 11
Outwood Station to Lofthouse and Stanley

Walk length 5.9 miles (9.5 km), of which 4 miles (6.5 km) is Wakefield Way. Field and riverside paths and a long stretch of disused railway.

By train: From Wakefield and Leeds to Outwood Station.

By car: Park at Outwood Station. For the main car-park drive down Lingwell Court on the Leeds side of the road bridge over the railway, but for a smaller, quieter car-park, turn down Railway Terrace at the Wakefield end of the bridge and follow it to its end.

Go down the steps leading to the platform for trains to Wakefield. At the bottom walk forward and take the path to the right of the metal fence. Follow this fence for some considerable distance, until the track turns right over a wide wooden bridge. *As you walk along, the land on your right was the site of the former Lofthouse Colliery, the site of a tragic disaster in the 1970s, when a number of miners lost their lives.* Having crossed the bridge, you are immediately faced by a fork: take the broad track climbing the slope. *At the top the M1 can be seen and heard in the distance on the left, and Ferrybridge Power Station is visible, though many miles away, ahead on the horizon.*

Drop downhill, cross a ditch and a cross-track, **and bear left on a narrow path through the trees to cross a bridge over a beck, here joining the Wakefield Way. Now the path is fenced and leads uphill in a deep hollow way. It is much used by horses and can be very muddy. Over the brow of the hill and descending slightly you cross a golfers' track and continue along the fenced path, passing under power lines. The path bends left and passes between houses to reach a street. Turn right. In a short distance at the road junction keep straight ahead, and at the next fork in the road keep right (Westgate Lane). At**

an interesting street name

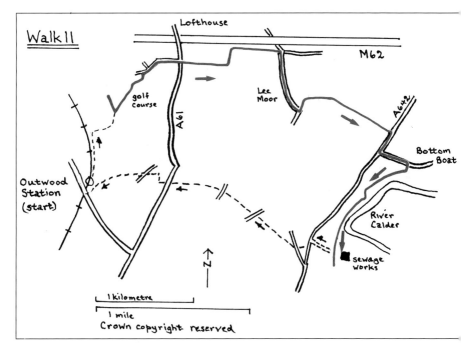

Walk 11

Lofthouse

M62

golf course

Lee Moor

A61

A642

Bottom Boat

Outwood Station (start)

River Calder

sewage works

N

1 kilometre

1 mile

Crown copyright reserved

the A61 Wakefield-Leeds road cross straight over and go through the wide gate opposite. Soon the track has a hedge on the left.

The hedge ends and is succeeded by a fence. Where this fence turns left, keep with it on a track heading towards the M62. At the motorway embankment turn right. When the track turns right again, keep forward with the fence on your left. You are now at a lower level than the motorway. The path crosses a beck and bears right to join a track. Turn left along it. On reaching the road (B6135) cross the stile and turn right, in a few yards keeping right again at the fork, along Lee Moor Lane. Where the road turns sharp right (Lee Moor Road), turn left along Fenton Road, a broad track. Where it ends, go through the stile by the gate ahead and bear right with the hedge on your right. At the end of this field cross the stile in the corner and continue by the hedge on your right. When the hedge turns right, keep straight forward across the middle of this large field, passing to the left of a wooden power line pole, and follow the path to its junction with the A642.

Cross the road and turn right. Opposite the Spindle Tree turn left down Bottom Boat Road following signs for the Trans Pennine Trail Bottom Boat North. A short way down ignore the TPT forking left to Methley North along St Peter's Crescent. Opposite Bottom Boat Post

46

Office (red telephone kiosk) and just past a converted chapel on the right, turn right (TPT Stanley South). Immediately before the car park at William Lamb's factory/offices the path turns right through a stile by a gate and heads across the field towards a large pylon. *The twin towers of St Peter's Church are clearly seen straight ahead. Shortly after passing the pylon on the right, the sweep of the River Calder, as it meanders from Wakefield to its confluence with the Aire at Castleford, will come into view on the left. Beyond the river can be seen the banks of the Aire & Calder Navigation, still a working waterway though much reduced in importance since the expansion of road transport.*

The path picks up a hedge on the left and then a high wall with houses. On reaching a tarmac drive, cross the entrance into Lake Yard and follow the wall on the left, but soon you turn right along the field edge. Follow the bank of the Calder for a short distance. Cross a footbridge and bear right with the metal fence of the Water Treatment Works to your left. When you reach the access road to the Works, leave the Wakefield Way, which goes straight ahead, *[To continue with the route of the WW, jump to p.48]* and turn right along the road. When you reach the busy A642, cross it with great care and turn left. In a short distance take a concrete track on the right. Keep forward along the edge of the green until you reach the next main road.

Cross over and bear right along the old railway track. Essentially you will follow it all the way back to Outwood. Cross straight over the first road you come to. Ignore two tarmac paths forking left. At the next fork, where the tarmac path bears right, keep straight forward up the grit track. At the top of the slope the track bears left to a road. Cross over, but ignoring the gate ahead, turn left, cross the end of Langdale Avenue and bear right, back up onto the old railway track.

Cross straight over the next road. After a time you climb some steps to reach the A61. Cross it and turn right, but at the next street on the left turn sharp left, down more steps, to rejoin the railway track. Shortly the way ahead is barred by a fence. Here you must leave the railway track. Turn right along a fenced footpath. Soon you are joined by another from the right. The path bears left. Cross the next road diagonally left to the signposted tarmac path opposite. Join a road coming in from the right and keep forward along it. Pass round a metal barrier across the road. The road bends right to reach another metal barrier. Immediately after it turn left over a stile by a gate along a broad track.

Soon there are football pitches on your right and trees on your left. At a clear fork in the path keep left, soon dropping down some steps. Cross a footbridge and then a stile to reach a car-park. Turn right. Soon there is access to Outwood Station *(trains to Wakefield from this side)* on the right.

Walk 12
Stanley

Walk length 3.88 miles (6.25 km), of which Wakefield Way is 0.93 miles (1.5 km). A varied stroll, mainly on field paths and tracks.

By bus: 443/444 Wakefield-Leeds (every 15 mins) to Lime Pit Lane, Stanley. Walk up Lime Pit Lane.

By car: Park at the Stanley Marsh Nature Reserve, found by following the A642 Wakefield-Oulton road. Turn left into Lime Pit Lane (signposted to Lee Moor, Lofthouse Gate and Outwood), proceed for 200 yards, pass the renovated property on the left and immediately after it park in the reserve car-park on the left. Return to Lime Pit Lane and turn left.

Follow the footway with the grassy area and football pitch on your right. Turn right into Oak Avenue and follow the path along the edge of the green. Where the tarmac path bears left, keep straight on along the concrete track to reach the A642. Turn left for about 60 yards, then cross the busy main road with great care and take the tarmac lane which forks off it (signposted as a PF). This is the access road to the Stanley Waste Water Treatment Works. Just before the entrance into the Works, turn right into the field, **here joining the Wakefield Way, and walk along with the hedge on your left.**

When the hedge/fence turns left, keep forward across the field towards the farm, joining a tarmac access road on the way. Pass to the right of the bungalow and bear slightly right through the yard to a kissing-gate beside a large gate. Turn left along the track, an old railway line *("The Nagger Line"),* **signposted TPT Stanley Ferry South. When you reach the next road, cross straight over into the driveway to The Mill House and walk towards the pub building. Pass to the right of the pub, follow the tarmac road as it bends right, walk along the left hand edge of the car-park and bear left up to the canal.**

By the early 1800s, the River Calder was no longer fordable and a horse and boat ferry was introduced (hence the name "Stanley Ferry") until replaced by a road bridge. The Aire and Calder Navigation provided an important transport link with Wakefield from the 18th century, enabling 40 tons of coal to be conveyed in boats called Tom Puddings, towed by steam tugs. The waterway was improved by the opening in 1839 of the first suspension aqueduct in the world. During its construction excavations at Stanley Ferry unearthed a Bronze Age boat. Roman coins have also been found in the area.

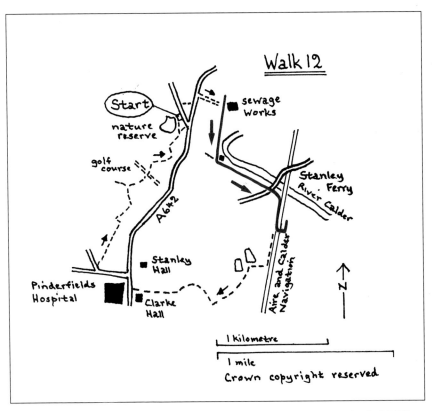

Walk 12

Start
nature reserve
golf course
A642
sewage works
Stanley Ferry
River Calder
Pinderfields Hospital
Stanley Hall
Clarke Hall
Aire and Calder Navigation
N

1 Kilometre
1 mile
Crown copyright reserved

Follow the canal to a footbridge. Here we leave the Wakefield Way, which crosses the bridge, *[To continue with the route of the WW, jump to p.51]* and keep on by the canal. In about 300 yards fork right through the hedge on a tarmac path leading to a metal kissing-gate. Follow the path towards a large pylon, with a lake on the right. Pass to the right of the pylon and soon reach another metal kissing-gate which leads onto a track. Turn right over a sleeper bridge. Ahead is another lake, popular with anglers: turn left along its bank.

Soon a fenced path leads towards houses. Follow it to the right round the outside of the estate. Where it bears left there is a good view right to Stanley Hall, the large house, *built about 1802 for the cloth merchant Benjamin Heywood and now the Wakefield Hospice.* Follow the path all the way up to the A642, one section between high hawthorn hedges being particularly attractive. Turn left along the footway, then just past the bus stop turn left again down the drive of the red brick 16th-17th century Clarke Hall, *one of Wakefield's finest houses, which groups of schoolchildren visit to experience life as it was lived in older times.* Having had a look at the outside of the house, return to the main road, cross it at the pedestrian lights and turn right past the entrance to Pinderfields Hospital.

Take the next street on the left (Bar Lane) and follow it as far as the next road on the right (Ouchthorpe Lane). About 20 yards along this, fork right down a signposted footpath. On reaching a field, keep down the left hand edge, but when the hedge on the left turns left, keep straight forward, passing to the right of a wooden telegraph pole, then bearing left along the bottom edge of the field. A few yards along go through a gap in the hedge on the right into an enclosed path. At the bottom of the fields the path turns left, and when it forks, turn left with a wall on the right.

Pass through a kissing-gate into the grounds of Normanton Golf Club. Hatfeild Hall, now the clubhouse, is visible over the wall. When the wall ends, turn right along a track. Follow this as far as a tarmac drive and cross straight over into the woods. The path soon crosses a plank bridge: bear right along the next path. Go straight over a golfers' path and a few yards further on keep left at a fork. Pass through a kissing-gate and follow the clear path ahead, in a few yards keeping right, i.e. straight on, at a fork.

A few yards before another kissing-gate leads out onto Lime Pit Lane, turn left and climb the slope for a view of the lake. You are now in the Stanley Marsh Nature Reserve. The path descends again by steps and crosses a board-walk. A short distance along turn right (or keep straight on if you are feeling energetic, maybe to walk round the lake) to reach the car-park on Lime Pit Lane. Leave it and turn right to return to the A642 and the buses.

THE BRONTË WAY

The Brontë Way is a long-distance footpath of some 69 kilometres/43 miles from Oakwell Hall, Birstall, near Leeds in West Yorkshire to Gawthorpe Hall, Padiham in Lancashire. It links together a variety of places which played a part in the lives and literary productions of the Brontë family, embracing paths which must have been used by the Reverend Patrick Brontë as he went about his ministry and others used by his daughters when they were visiting friends or taking walks in the countryside which inspired their novels. It also offers an attractive introduction to the pastoral and moorland landscapes of the South Pennines.

The route is fully described and illustrated in the form of eleven circular walks in Marje Wilson's *The Brontë Way,* published by the Ramblers' Association, West Riding Area at £4.50 and obtainable from the Publishers at 27 Cookridge Avenue, Leeds LS16 7NA (please add 80p for post and packing).

Walk 13
Stanley Ferry to Altofts and Kirkthorpe

Length of walk 6.83 miles (11 km), of which Wakefield Way is 1.86 miles (3 km). A peaceful stretch of canal towpath is followed by a traverse of Altofts and easy walking past the ruined Newfield Hall and along the Calder to the old hamlet of Kirkthorpe, from where the route returns by more canal towpath to the start. The walk starts at the car-park of the Stanley Ferry Marina.

By bus: 125/147 Wakefield-Pontefract bus to Stanley Ferry.

By car: Park in the car-park at Stanley Ferry Marina.

Follow the tarmac road to the right of the pub. It bends right. Walk along the left hand edge of the car park and bear left up to the canal. Turn right along the towpath as far as the first footbridge over it (Ramsdens Bridge).

Cross over the canal, turn left and proceed towards the cottages *constructed for canal workers in the early 19th century.* **Stay on the path between the cottages and the canal and head for the pedestrian footbridge over the Calder.** *There are now two aqueducts carrying the canal over the river. The original (1839) cast iron structure, the first suspension aqueduct to be built anywhere in the world, was complemented in 1981 by a new concrete channel in order to reduce wear and tear on the older one. Not long after this, trade all but vanished from the canal. Do not attempt to walk along the aqueducts.* **Keep to the path over the footbridge and then follow the canal under the road bridge. (There are steps leading to and from the Stanley-Altofts road at this point.)**

Follow the towpath past Birkwood Lock, where it widens and becomes a tarmac road. Follow this road until about 100 yards before the next lock (King's Road Lock) steps on the right lead down to a stile. *(A notice posted here by Rose Farm warns that this is not a recreation area for dogs.)* **Here you leave the Wakefield Way.** *[To continue with the route of the WW, jump to p.55]*

Cross the stile and walk straight forward across the field to the next stile, then follow the fence on the right to the next one and walk straight up the next field to the houses at the top. The next stile is just to the left of a large gate. Walk on up the broad grassy track and the following street. Cross the next main road diagonally right and take the signposted footpath with the school on the left. Shortly after the end of the school

Walk 13

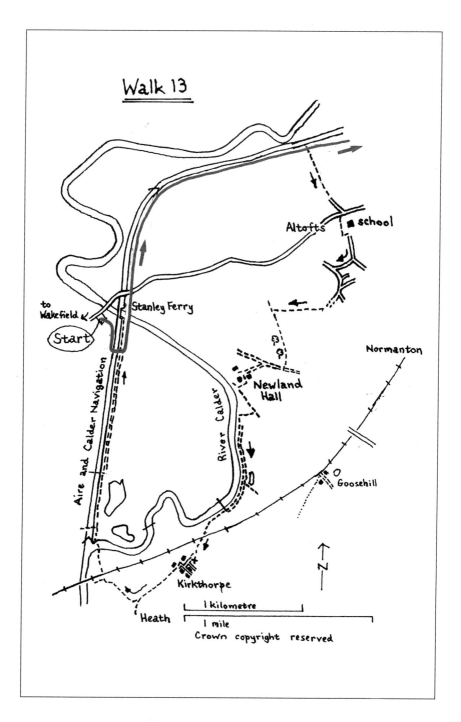

to Wakefield

Start

Stanley Ferry

Altofts

school

Aire and Calder Navigation

River Calder

Newland Hall

Normanton

Goosehill

Kirkthorpe

Heath

N

1 kilometre

1 mile

Crown copyright reserved

grounds the path turns sharp left. Turn right along the next street. Pass a small green in the middle of the street and at the next main road turn right, passing the Lee Brigg pub. Cross the road when convenient, and immediately after Lee Brigg infant school turn left along Patience Lane. Shortly after Drury Lane comes in from the left keep right at the fork. When the tarmac ends, pass round the large gate ahead into a hedged track.

The track narrows to a footpath. Having passed under the power lines, you reach a T-junction of paths. Turn left towards the wood. The path passes to the left of the wood. At the end of the wood you reach Newfield Lane, a cross track. To continue following the bridleway you should go a few yards to the right and then turn left along an old hedgerow, but this section has at present been diverted due to opencast mining. So turn to the right and walk along Newfield Lane. When the track forks, keep left towards the ruined Newfield Hall. Immediately after passing a derelict brick barn on the left, turn left up a track which passes to the left of another ruined building. At the top of the slope the track bends right, and after passing more ruins it bends left again, where a path comes in from the right.

Down to the right, glimpsed through the trees, is the River Calder. The track narrows to a path and you reach a fork. Keep right, through a plantation of young birches. Shortly another path comes in from the left. In a few yards at a fork keep right, down into the woods. At the next fork keep left, and the River Calder is close by to the right. Pass under a concrete bridge over the river to reach a gravel track. Bear right along it. This good track leads parallel to the river almost all the way to Kirkthorpe. After passing a small lake on the left, keep straight on at a signposted footpath junction. Just after passing a pipeline over the river the track narrows to a footpath. Pass under a railway bridge and bear right with the tarmac track up to Kirkthorpe.

On reaching the houses the lane turns left, then right, and passes to the right of the church. *This is a delightful secluded spot.* Enter the churchyard by steps near the road junction and walk past the main door to the east end. *The gravestones with large incised crosses commemorate nine Benedictine nuns who escaped the French Revolution in 1792 and lived at Heath Hall between 1811-21.* Leave the churchyard by the main gate and turn right, passing the end of Half Moon Lane. *On the right are the village stocks. Behind them and to the left are Frieston's Hospital Almshouses.* Turn back and walk down Half Moon Lane. *Notice the old Cheesecake Inn on the right, dated 1740. On the left is the back view of the hospital, where a plaque informs us that it was founded in 1595 by John Frieston of Altofts. Below it is the old schoolhouse, built in 1899.*

Turn left at the next junction, along an unsurfaced track which soon narrows to a footpath. After a short distance you can either stay on the higher path or go down steps on the right for a closer look at Half Moon Pond, on the former course of the River Calder and popular with anglers. This lower variant rejoins the main path further on. When you reach a major fork, keep right through the barrier. After dropping into a dip the path climbs a low embankment: turn right along the top of this. Follow it until you are level with a tunnel under the railway on the right, then drop steeply down and go through the tunnel. Follow the path to Blue Bridge and cross the River Calder.

From the bridge walk forward until you reach a cross track. Turn left for a yard or two, but don't cross the canal bridge: instead fork right down onto the path beside the canal. Follow this along, passing under the next bridge, and there joining a tarmac road. Cross the canal by the next bridge, which you will recognise as Ramsdens Bridge, which you used at the start of the walk. Retrace your steps past the pub to the car-park.

an unusual seat at Newmillerdam

54

Walk 14
Normanton Station to Castleford Station

A linear walk of 5.9 miles (9.5 km), of which 4.35 miles (7 km) are Wakefield Way, almost entirely by canal and river. Return to Normanton by train (usually hourly).

By train: Wakefield (Kirkgate) to Normanton (Hallam Line).

By car: Normanton Station car-park is free; the car-park by the Lidl supermarket nearby is pay-and-display.

Walk up the station access road, and on reaching the T-junction turn sharp left along the footpath, with the Lidl supermarket and car-park on your right. At the next road turn left over the railway bridge, cross the road when the footway starts on the other side and take the first track on the right, which leads to the left of a farm and narrows to a footpath between fields. Just before you reach the next houses turn left along a cross path between hedges. Cross over two streets and when your way ahead is blocked by a wall turn right along another ginnel. At the next street keep forward to pass to the left of the parish church of St. Mary Magdalene, Altofts, cross the road ahead and turn left.

Pass the Horse and Jockey and opposite the Martin Frobisher Infant School turn right down Hillcrest. At the end keep forward along the broad grassy track between houses to cross a stile into a field. Walk straight down the field to the next stile, then follow the fence on your left to the next one. Keep straight on over the next field to a stile in the hedge. Climb the steps to the canal towpath and turn right along it.

You have now joined the Wakefield Way, and essentially you are going to follow the towpath by the canal and the River Calder all the way to Castleford. Follow the tarmac lane past King's Road Lock, but where it rises to join a road, fork left off it and follow the towpath under the road bridge. Join a lane, pass under the M62 and continue along the towpath. After a time the canal forks and you follow the old cut to pass under the Leeds-Normanton railway bridge. You can no longer walk past the next lock, where the old cut joined the River Calder, as a new wharf has been built by Lafarge Aggregates, so you must fork right up a pebble track with a green metal fence on the left. Follow this fence past the entrance into the wharf, and soon you bear right over a concrete bridge. Turn left to re-join the river bank. The riverside path passes under two railway bridges and a modern road bridge, then through the yard of Methley Bridge Boat Club to a

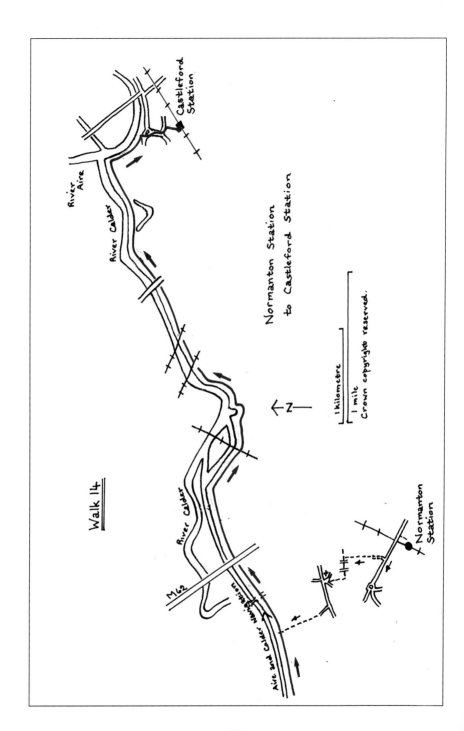

Walk 14

River Aire

River Calder

River Calder

M62

Aire and Calder

Normanton Station
to Castleford Station

Castleford Station

Normanton Station

N

1 kilometre
1 mile
Crown copyrights reserved.

stile/kissing-gate which gives access to the flood bank of the river. Walk along this until you reach a stile. Cross and fork left off the flood bank to another stile. Over this you have a high fence on your right. Pass the confluence of the Calder and the Aire and keep on by the river (now, of course, the Aire!) until your way is blocked by a brick wall. Turn right to the road, cross straight over, pass through the bollards and walk up the street opposite, to pass to the left of Castleford Parish Church. Cross the main road with great care, and immediately after the New Junction pub turn left along Carlton Street, cross it and turn right through arches in the row of shops, then walk forward along the paved way to Castleford Station. The Wakefield Way continues straight on through the underpass under the railway *(To continue with the route of the WW, jump to p.58).*

Walk 15
Castleford Station to Pontefract Bus Station

A linear walk of 3.42 miles (5.5 km), all of it Wakefield Way. A brief traverse of Castleford and a country lane lead over the M62 to Pontefract racecourse and through Pontefract streets to the bus station. Return to the start by bus (134/135/136/137, frequent).

By train: *Wakefield (Kirkgate)/Leeds to Castleford.*

By car: *Park either in Castleford town centre or in the car-park at Pontefract Park. In this case follow the last part of the route to Pontefract bus station, take a bus to Castleford and walk back to the car.*

Turn left out of Castleford Station, then left again to go through the underpass under the railway. Walk straight up the next street (Beancroft Road), which becomes Barnes Road. Shortly after passing a small park on the left, the road climbs to a T-junction. Cross over the road ahead and turn right. Immediately after the level crossing at Cutsyke Junction turn left along a road signposted as a cycle route to Pontefract Park.

It is not long before the M62 can be heard and seen ahead. **After a time the tarmac surface ends. Ignore a track forking left, then a short distance further on just before a house turn left along a signposted bridleway, soon passing round a metal barrier. The track turns left when it reaches the M62, then soon turns right to cross the motorway by a bridge. On the other side turn left and keep left at the fork, parallel to the motorway. After a time the track bends right away from the motorway, but shortly turns left again.**

At the far end of a wood on the right of the track turn sharp right on a track which leads along the outside rails of Pontefract racecourse. *Racing at Pontefract was first recorded in the 1720s. The grandstand was built in 1802.* **Shortly before you reach the marker post for furlong 3 a footpath comes in from the right, there is a waymark post and an old metal gate. On race days you will have to stay on the track, which leads behind the grandstand and comes to a metal barrier. Here the walk route turns right along the tarmac road,** *but if you cross straight over it and follow the outside of the rails round you will reach the access road to the car-park with toilets and a little further on the children's playground and the boating lake.*

On non-race days turn left to duck under the barrier and cross the racecourse, duck under the next rail then bear right to pick up a

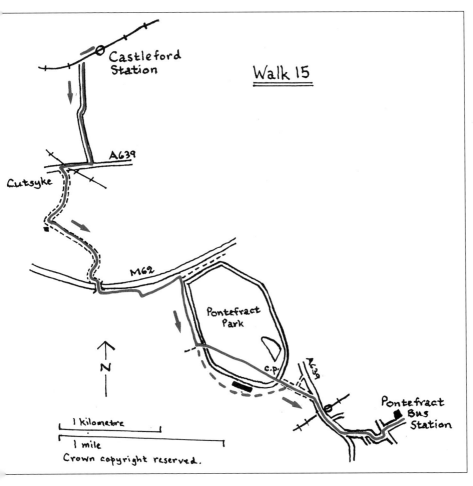

Walk 15

Castleford Station

A639

Cutsyke

M62

Pontefract Park

N

c.p.

A639

Pontefract Bus Station

1 Kilometre

1 mile

Crown copyright reserved.

faint path heading over the grass towards the grandstand. Pass the curious little race results building to reach the car park and toilets. Take the path passing to the right of the car-park, pass round a metal barrier, cross over the access road to the car-park - the children's play-ground is on the left - and at the next cross path either turn left for the boating lake or right to continue the walk by crossing the racecourse again and joining the car-park access road. Turn left along it.

Both routes meet at a mini-roundabout. Keep forward past the old gateposts and along the wide metalled drive which was once the main entrance to the course to emerge by traffic lights at the junction of Park Lane and the main (A639) road. Cross the main road

RACECOURSE

Organised Horse Races have taken place in this Park since at least the 18th century. The Course was extended in 1983 to form the longest circular flat racecourse in Europe and probably in the world.

at the pelican crossing and turn right along the dual carriageway, over the railway line (Tanshelf Station), up the hill and round the left-hand bend. As the dual carriageway starts to bend right, take the road to the left (Front Street/Cornmarket).

The Tap and Barrel pub is on the right followed by the Sessions House (1807) on the left. At the end of Cornmarket there is a toilet block on the left opposite the war memorial. Walk on down Beastfair and turn left into the Market Place, pass the Buttercross, *"erected in 1734 to shelter people selling dairy produce"* according to the blue plaque inside, and proceed to the Georgian Town Hall at the far end. Turn left and then sharp right into Bridge Street and Horsefair. The bus station is about 100 yards down Horsefair on the left-hand side *(To continue with the route of the WW, jump to p.62).*

Long Lane above Carleton village (page 64)

Walk 16
Pontefract Bus Station to East Hardwick

A linear walk of 5 miles (8 km), which is entirely Wakefield Way. Return to the start by bus.

By bus: *No. 248 Pontefract -South Elmsall-Upton (Mon.-Sat. usually half-hourly) passes along the A639 through East Hardwick.*

By car: *Park courteously on Darrington Road in East Hardwick, walk to the A639, cross and turn right to the bus stop for a bus to Pontefract bus station.*

Leave the bus station and turn left down Horsefair. When the main road bends right down to traffic lights, keep straight forward to pass Micklegate Methodist church and the Old Castle pub and reach the gates of Pontefract Castle. *The castle was originally built soon after the Norman Conquest and is well worth a visit (free entry). It was demolished after the Civil War, having witnessed the murder of Richard II in 1400.* **To the right of the castle entrance a flagged path descends alongside the castle grounds to join a cobbled street. When this forks, keep right.** *On the left just before the main road are the foundations of an Anglo-Saxon church.* **Cross the main road to what appears to be a ruined church.** *In fact within these "ruins" there is a newer brick structure still providing a place of worship. A notice above the door reads "All Saints: the ancient parish church of Pontefract. The present building 13th to 15th century, ruined in 1645 during Civil War... noted for double helix staircase. Sketched by Turner."*

Pass to the left of the church and at the next main road (A645) turn left. Follow the footway along, passing under a railway bridge, and 60 yards after the start of the 40 m.p.h. limit fork left into a tarmac road, but immediately fork right off it towards the high metal fence of the Pontefract Sowgate Lane Waste Water Pumping Station. Bear left at the fence along Sowgate Lane. Follow this broad track through the fields and past Pear Tree Farm on the right. A few yards after the farm a footpath comes in from the left - the tunnel under the M62 is just over 100 yards ahead - and you turn right down the right hand edge of a field, parallel to the M62 a field's width away. Pass through a tunnel under the Rotherham-York/Selby railway and keep forward to the A645. Turn right for 40 yards and cross the road into a broad, grassy track with houses on the left (Lower Taythes Lane). Follow this track, for a time a quite deep hollow way, for some

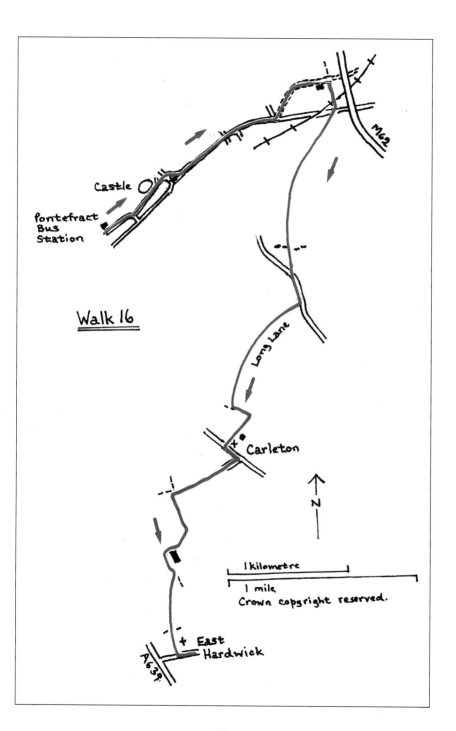

Castle

Pontefract
Bus
Station

M62

Walk 16

Long Lane

Carleton

N

1 kilometre

1 mile
Crown copyright reserved.

East
Hardwick

A639

considerable distance. Ignore a track coming in from the right and another forking off left and soon your track bends right to join a road (Street Furlong Lane). Turn left. About 40 yards after the entrance into Baghill Nurseries on the left, take a track on the right through the fields (Long Lane). When you reach an avenue of trees on a low ridge, a path comes in from the right. Bear left with a hedge on your right. Where the hedge turns right, stay with it, and descend a sunken lane. Follow the track past Church Farm, and at Carleton Parish Church turn right, then left to reach the main road.

Turn left past the church for 200 yards to Moor Lane on the right. This is at first a tarmac estate road, but then continues as an unmade track. Follow it until it makes a kink and crosses a beck. Turn left here along a cross path with the beck on your left. After a time the path bends right, then bears right again along the perimeter fence of the Carleton Waste Water Treatment Works. At the end of the fence turn left, cross the access road, a large pipe and a footbridge and continue along the perimeter fence. This is succeeded by another high fence. After a time you turn right over a footbridge and a stile into a field. Cross the field diagonally left to the far corner. aiming for East Hardwick parish church. Cross a stile and a footbridge and follow the now very clear path in the same direction across the next field. At the end of this continue along the right of the hedge, pass the church on the left and join Darrington Road in the village of East Hardwick *(To continue the route of the WW, jump to p.65).*

(To continue the route of the WW, jump to p.65).

The Wakefield Way turns left here, but to return to Pontefract turn right, walk to the A639, cross it and turn right to the bus stop.

Walk 17
East Hardwick and Ackworth

A circular walk of 4.97 miles (8 km), of which 1.4 miles (2.25 km) is Wakefield Way. An easy, flat ramble through lovely countryside. It starts and finishes in East Hardwick.

By bus: No. 246 Pontefract-Barnsley, 248 Pontefract-South Elmsall-Upton pass along the A639 through East Hardwick. After alighting walk back a few yards and turn right past the old pump along Darrington Road as far as Church Lane, where you pick up the Wakefield Way

By car: Park considerately on Darrington Road in East Hardwick.

Begin the walk by proceeding along Darrington Road in the opposite direction to the A639. Where the road begins to curve left take the bridleway on the right, an unsurfaced track. In a little more than 200 yards cross a stile by a gate on the right and follow the hedge on your right along. Where it ends, keep straight on over the field to a stile onto the A639. Turn left along this busy road (there is no footway, but there is a broad verge) for just over 200 yards, then take the lane forking right (Whitegates Lane). When you reach the entrance into a house, fork left. Cross straight over the next motor road and follow the concrete road opposite. *Shortly before you reach the Ackworth Water Treatment Works a stone on the left informs you "Here ends Ackworth Bridle Road".*

    Pass the entrance into the works and follow the track to the concrete bridge over the River Went. *Notice the old stone packhorse bridge (Burnhill Bridge) just to the left of it.* **The Wakefield Way turns left at this point.** *[To continue with the route of the WW, jump to p.68]*

    Don't cross the bridge, but turn right along a footpath with the river to your left. There now follows a long stretch of pleasant riverside path. Having passed under a high railway viaduct keep on by the river. Pass a concrete bridge and continue along the track. At a fork keep right, ignoring a footbridge, stile and the continuation of the riverside path. The path/track leads to Low Ackworth, and on reaching the houses it becomes a tarmac street. When you reach the main road turn right.

    The road makes a long curve left, but where it begins to curve right, just after a bus shelter, post box and telephone kiosk, fork left up Westfield Grove. The track soon bends left and you reach a stile by a gate on the right. Walk straight over the field to the stile opposite, then on by the left hand edge of the next field to the next stile. Over it turn sharp left, still with

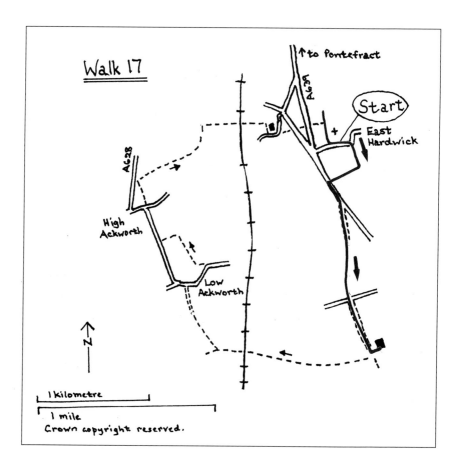

Walk 17

↑ to Pontefract

Start

East Hardwick

A639

A628

High Ackworth

Low Ackworth

N

1 kilometre

1 mile

Crown copyright reserved.

the fence/hedge on your left, to a stile and a minor road. Turn right and follow the road (Lee Lane) to High Ackworth. On reaching a T-junction, cross straight over to the stile opposite and follow the hedge/fence on your left.

When the fence turns left keep straight forward across the field to the far hedge. Do not go down the steps onto the A628, but walk back over the field, at right angles to the path you have just arrived on. On the far side pass through the hedge and cross a footbridge, then keep along the right hand edge of the next field. At its end there is another footbridge, then keep forward again along the field boundary. Cross another footbridge at the end of this field and turn sharp left with a hedge to your left. When the hedge ends at a field corner, turn right, keeping the field boundary on your left, and follow it round until a clear path heads off right across the middle of the field making for a footbridge in the distance.

66

Follow the path across two fields to this bridge and cross it, then keep forward along the track.

When you reach the houses of Hundhill, follow the boundary fence round to the right, to cross a stile onto Hundhill Lane. Turn left, but when the road bends left go through the gap-stile in the wall ahead and follow the fenced path to the next road. Turn left for a few yards to a stile on the right, and follow the hedge on your left to the next stile, then walk forward to the A639. Cross straight over to the footpath signpost opposite, then walk straight over the field. At the far side turn right along an old hedged track which leads back to East Hardwick.

East Hardwick Church

Walk 18
Thorpe Audlin and Upton

Length of walk 7 miles (11.25 km), of which 3.73 miles (6 km) is Wakefield Way. Easy walking through attractive, open countryside.

By bus: *246 Pontefract-Barnsley, 248/249 Pontefract-Upton, 485 Wakefield-Doncaster to The Upton Centre on Waggon Lane, then walk back towards the centre of Upton.*

By car: *A large (but unsigned) car-park has been laid out for access to the reclaimed Upton Colliery site on Waggon Lane, Upton. Park here, walk back to the entrance of the car-park and turn left.*

Where Waggon Lane bends left, there is a memorial stone on the right to the miners who lost their lives at Upton Colliery 1926-64 in a small garden. Pass behind the stone onto the road and cross it diagonally left onto a track, in a few yards turning right up the hedged footpath signposted to Thorpe Audlin. Cross straight over a street and continue up the path. When you reach a junction with a high metal fence ahead, turn left along the track with the fence on your right. The track becomes a street - the water tower is prominent to your right - which leads to a main road. Turn right.

When the road begins to bend left fork right off it into Manor View, but in a yard or two fork left along a hedged bridleway. Upton Beacon is to your right, and there are fine views left and ahead as you emerge from the hedged lane. Badsworth is down on your left and Thorpe Audlin ahead and slightly to the right, with Pontefract the town in the distance. Ignore a path forking right and keep forward through the fields. The clear path leads in time to a stile by a large white gate: cross and take the path slightly left ahead, to pass to the left of Rogerthorpe Manor, *built around 1600 and now a country house hotel.*

Cross a stile by a gate onto a road - *Badsworth is a short distance along to the left* - and cross straight over into the track opposite (Owler's Lane). After a time ignore a track coming in from the left (Firthfield Lane) and keep on along what is now Burnhill Lane. After a time you reach two bridges side by side over the River Went, a wide concrete one and the narrow, packhorse Burnhill Bridge. Cross and turn right over a small clapper bridge, **here joining the Wakefield Way.** *Ackworth Water Treatment Works are to your left.*

Cross another small footbridge and follow the riverside path until another footbridge enables you to cross the river. A clear path leads

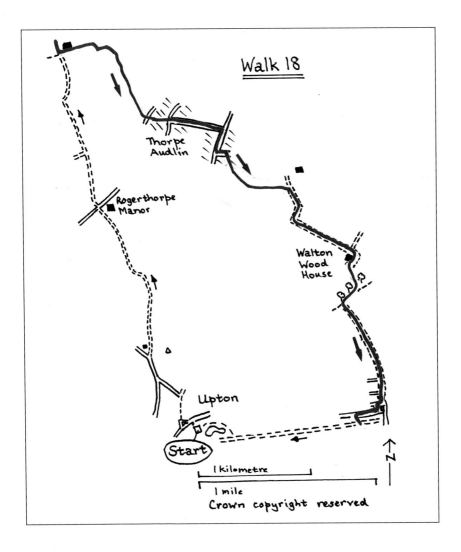

Walk 18

Thorpe
Audlin

Rogerthorpe
Manor

Walton
Wood
House

Upton

Start

1 kilometre

1 mile

Crown copyright reserved

straight ahead through the fields. On reaching the houses of Thorpe Audlin, follow the track through between them, cross straight over the next road into a grassy track, which leads to a main road (B6474). Cross over and walk along Darning Lane. At a crossroads turn right along Causeway Garth Lane, past Thorpe Manor (over the wall on your left). Follow the tarmac lane as it bends left, and just past a house called The Orchard turn right along a signposted footpath between gardens.

At the end keep forward through a small wood to reach a

footbridge and stile. Cross and walk straight over the next field to the next stile, then bear slightly left over the next field to the next stile. You enter a large field with no apparent path. Either turn left and follow the hedge (which is the right of way) or find a tractor track about five yards into the field and turn left along this, keeping parallel to the hedge. Near the top of the slope turn left round a small wood, still probably on the tractor track, still parallel to the hedge. When the remains of the hedge end, bear half right, then shortly the track turns left for a few yards to join a track coming from the farm to the left. Turn right on this with a hedge on your right. Cross the beck at the end of the field and bear right with the track, still with a hedge on your right. Pass through a wide gap in the hedge ahead and turn left, now with a hedge on the left.

Soon you cross the grassy runway of Walton Wood airfield. Cross straight over the entrance drives to Walton Wood Dovecote and Walton Wood House onto a track which bears right to pass behind Walton Wood House. Where the high hedge on the right turns right, turn left and walk up the right hand edge of the field to Walton Wood. Follow the path into the wood: it bends right, crosses a cross path and climbs to the top edge of the wood. Turn right here along the track, but in a short distance turn left onto another track (Sheepwalk Lane). On reaching the houses, pass the ends of two streets on the right and continue until the track reaches a main road on a bend. Turn right along it, but take the first street on the left (Barnsdale Way). Immediately it forks: keep right.

Between houses no.45 and 47 take the footpath on the left, pass round the barrier, cross the concrete bridge and climb steeply up the embankment onto an old railway track. The Wakefield Way crosses this and drops down the embankment on the other side, *[To continue with the route of the WW, jump to p.74]* but we turn right along the old track. When you reach a fork, either keep left on the narrower path to follow the old track or go right and follow the hedge on your left along. The track passes through a deep cutting and then is forced to go right as a former bridge is missing, to link up with the other path. Turn left, cross the shallow dip and take the broad track up the other side. Soon you are back on the old railway track.

Presently you are once more in a deep cutting. When you emerge from it, leave the track by going through the barrier on the right into the Upton Colliery Reclamation Area. Immediately fork left, cross a bridge and walk anti-clockwise round the lake, either on the lower or the higher path. Both lead back to the car-park. Bear right through the car-park to regain Waggon Lane and the bus stops.

Pontefract Butter Cross (page 60)

Walk 19
South and North Elmsall and Wrangbrook

Length of walk 6.83 miles (11 km), of which 2.8 miles (4.5 km) is Wakefield Way. The walk, which includes attractive reclaimed colliery land and open arable countryside, starts and finishes at South Elmsall Station. *N.B. Sections of the route at Wrangbrook and North Elmsall will be affected by the construction of the Hemsworth to A1 Link Road.*

By train: to South Elmsall (Metro train Wakefield Line).

By car: car-park at South Elmsall Station.

Climb the steps to leave South Elmsall Station and turn right along the road. Start climbing the hill and take the first street on the left, passing Trinity Methodist Church. Now take the second street on the left (Lower Northcroft). At the bottom of the hill follow the street as it bends right, and where it ends keep straight forward across the grass along the top of a low embankment towards a hedge corner. Pick up the hedge on your left and follow it to a path junction. Turn left over the footbridge and continue on the surfaced path. Do not cross the footbridge over the railway, but take the narrow path just to the right of it. This leads through light woodland, and after a time you must climb some steps to a road.

   Cross straight over and take the track opposite, in a few yards keeping left at a fork. The track leads along parallel to the railway. *After a time a railway bridge visible half left marks where the Wakefield-Moorthorpe-Sheffield line crosses the Wakefield-S.Elmsall-Doncaster line.* Soon, with the railway close by on the left, fork right down a long flight of steps and bear right along the track at the bottom, immediately crossing a beck by a bridge. The track follows the beck for a short distance, then bears right at the point where another track comes steeply down the banking on the left. Reach a T-junction with a large lake ahead and turn right, keeping the lake on your left. This is an attractive area of reclaimed former colliery land.

   Shortly after the end of the lake ignore a track forking left and another less clear one forking right. After a time you have a hedge/fence on your left, and where this ends at a track junction turn left. A little further on the track turns sharply right. Follow it all the way to the B6474. Cross diagonally left (care! blind bends!) to take the minor road opposite. On reaching the A638, cross and turn right, but in a few yards fork left into the village of North Elmsall. *Notice the old milestone by Milestone House on the right.* Pass the Victorian church of St.Margaret, and where the road swings right, keep straight on along the track, ignoring the stile on the left.

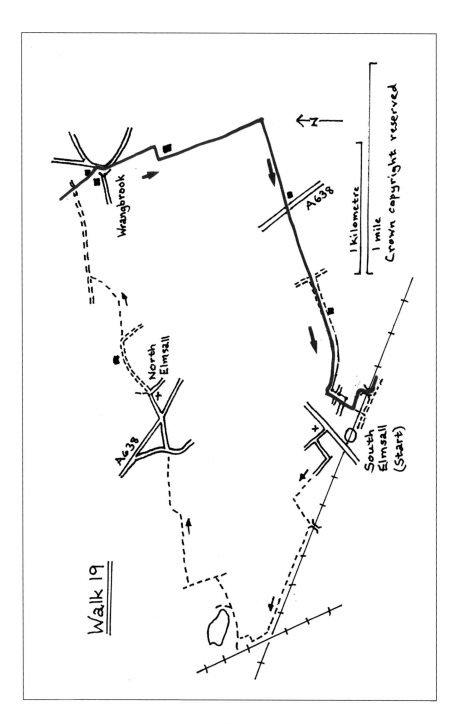

Walk 19

Wrangbrook

A638

North Elmsall

A638

South Elmsall (Start)

← N →

1 kilometre
1 mile

Crown copyright reserved

In a few yards pass through a gateway. The track leads past North Elmsall Hall and becomes tarmac. About 100 yards beyond the buildings fork left off the tarmac road onto a track leading to the crossing of a beck, but about ten yards before the beck there should be a tractor track forking right and running parallel to the beck (the bridleway actually runs beside the beck). Shortly after you pass under power lines a footpath crosses the track. Turn left along it, in a few yards crossing the beck by a clapper bridge and turning right along the edge of the next field, now parallel to the beck on your right. At the end of the field the path used to pass under a railway bridge, which has now gone, but pass through and immediately turn right.

In a few yards fork right through the hedge onto the old railway track and bear left along it. It runs here in a cutting. When a clear path comes in from the left, bear right, still on the old railway. After a time ignore a clear path forking down right off the embankment, but a few yards further on you reach a spot where a footpath crosses the line, coming steeply up from a barrier and concrete footbridge down on the left and descending steeply the embankment to the right. Take this path to the right, **here joining the Wakefield Way. Bear left at the bottom. The clear path leads through light woodland and reaches a cross path. Turn left, but in five yards fork right off this clear path along a narrow path which leads in a few yards to a stile. Cross and follow the path forward to another stile and a footbridge. Over this turn right along the track past Brookside Farm at Wrangbrook.**

On reaching the road, cross straight over (care! blind bend!) into Sleep Hill Lane opposite. In a few yards cross a stile in the fence on the right (just before a large gate) and follow a faint path through this long field close to the hedge on the left. Shortly before you reach a large pylon go through a gate in a cross fence and pass to the left of the pylon to reach a stile. Cross it and turn left along the track for a few yards to reach a much better track on a bend. Turn right along it.

At the next junction, with Upton Wrangbrook Waste Water Treatment Works ahead, turn right to pass Wrangbrook House and enter an old railway track. Soon bear left off the embankment down some steps and follow the fence on the left. At the corner turn left with it, and follow it until it turns sharp left again. Stay with it for three yards, then bear right away from it to cross a footbridge. Bear slightly right on a track up through the fields. At the top of the hill ignore a track forking right, keep straight on to pass under the power lines and walk along the narrow unploughed headland between two fields.

About 100 yards before you reach a group of trees ahead, and

when you are level with the start of a small wood about 200 yards across the field on the right, turn right across the field to the right hand edge of this small wood, pass to the right of it and follow the hedge on your left, and drop down to cross a ditch at a gap in a facing hedge, then continue down by the hedge on your left to the A638. Cross straight over, go down the steps and walk straight over the field to the hedge on the far side. Go down the concrete steps, cross a disused railway track, climb the steps on the other side, turn left along the field edge for 15 yards then turn right and cross the field to a hedge corner.

Walk along with the hedge on your right, following the field boundary to a junction of tracks. Keep straight forward, soon passing Quarry Farm. When you reach the houses of South Elmsall, keep forward along the road, which after a time turns left. At the crossroads keep straight forward down Hemings Way, but when this starts to bend right, fork left off it onto an unsurfaced track, which soon bends left. Shortly a concrete footpath crosses the track. The Wakefield Way goes straight on here, *[To continue with the route of the WW, jump to p.76]* but we turn right down the concrete path. Cross the footbridge over the railway and turn right to return to South Elmsall station.

canalside path

Walk 20
South Elmsall

Length of walk 6.37 miles (10.25 km), of which 2.5 miles (4 km) is Wakefield Way. A disused railway line, reclaimed colliery land and an old track through fine open countryside are encountered on this walk, which starts and finishes at South Elmsall Station.

By train: to South Elmsall (Metro train Wakefield Line). If you are arriving by train from Wakefield, you will need to cross the railway by the two sets of steps to reach the car-park.

By car: car-park at South Elmsall Station.

From the far end of the station car-park walk along the track, which soon becomes a tarmac road. Cross the railway by the first footbridge, walk up the concrete footpath and turn right along a cross track, **here joining the Wakefield Way. On reaching a track junction turn right and cross over the railway by the next bridge. Turn left along the tarmac road. This is an access road to the South Elmsall Waste Water Treatment Works, and when you reach the Works, turn right with the fence. When the fence turns sharp left, keep with it, and soon the path bends right away from the fence and crosses a footbridge.**

Turn left along the edge of the field, but in a short distance follow the path as it bends right to cross the field with a ditch on the right. On reaching the trees, ignore a concrete footbridge on the right and keep on up to join a disused railway track. Turn right along it and follow it until the track drops to a road. Here turn left along the road as far as a large metal gate on the right (beside Station House and opposite Moorhouse Lane on the left). Go through this (or pass round it) and walk up the track, but where the track bends left, fork right off it up a path which soon bends left.

The path leads along the continuation of the disused railway. Follow this as far as you can, until the path drops steeply down to a concrete track on the site of a former railway bridge (some redbrick masonry survives). Turn left along the concrete track, but immediately fork left off it along a signposted bridleway, past the two large blocks of stone, but in three yards turn right through the hedge, walk forward the short distance to the far side of the field and there bear left along the right hand edge of the field with a hedge on the right. At the end of the field the path enters a wood, but stays close to its right hand edge.

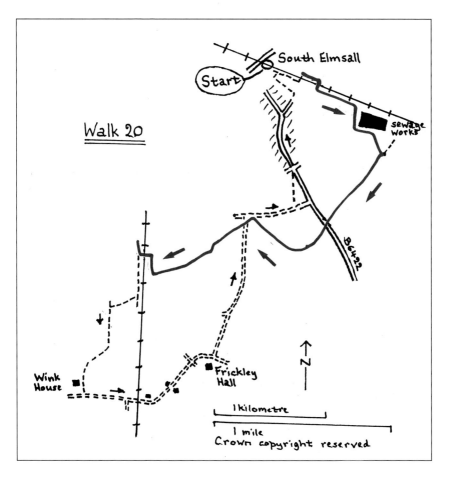

Walk 20

Leave the wood again to follow the right hand edge of the next field. At its end ignore a path forking left and a track on the right and keep forward over a low barrier and along the right hand edge of the next field on a clear track, soon joining an even better track coming from the right. Follow the track to a T-junction, with the embankment of the Wakefield-Moorthorpe-Sheffield railway straight ahead, and turn right. Shortly turn left to pass under the railway. On the far side the Wakefield Way turns right, *[To continue with the route of the WW, jump to p.81]* but we turn left.

Just after passing under the power lines fork right away from the railway on a track which passes to the left of a large pylon. The quality of the track deteriorates sharply, and it can be excessively muddy. When you reach a cross track, turn left along it. Soon you leave the wood *(and the*

77

Wakefield District: here you enter Doncaster) and follow the track straight across the field to the hedge on the far side. Pass through an old gateway in the hedge, and now you have a hedge on your left. The track soon bends right and rises, but where it passes through the hedge fork right off it and continue up with the hedge still on your left. Soon you will see a stile to the left of a large gate in the fence ahead. Cross and walk straight up the next field. Soon you will see the next stile also to the left of a large gate. Old paving stones start a few yards before it and lead to it.

Keep forward along the next long field, with the buildings of Wink House Farm to your right. Ignore a gate on the right out of the field. Cross the stile in the far corner - *the village of Clayton is half right across the fields* - and turn sharp left along a broad track. Ignore a track forking right, a few yards after which you once more cross the railway, this time far below you. After passing a stone-built house the track bends left and you pass through Frickley Home Farm. The road now becomes tarmac. Keep straight on at a crossroads - the road on the right leads to Frickley Hall, of which you will get a good view a little further on - but at the next road junction be sure to turn left. Pass through an old gateway, ignore a track to the left, and here the tarmac ends. A short distance further on ignore a track to the right. *By the time you pass under the power lines you have returned from Doncaster into Wakefield District.*

When you reach the junction with the concrete track (you have been here before), turn right along it. There are massive spoil heaps on the left. Follow the lane until you reach a metal barrier on the left (about 100 yards before a gate across the lane and a road). Go through the barrier and climb the bank of reclaimed land. At the top either turn right and follow the trees on your right all the way round or follow the track across the middle of the large expanse of grass, heading for some red roofs in the distance. On the far side drop to a barrier beside a gate and turn left along the road, keeping straight on at the mini-roundabout.

Cross the main road where convenient and turn right immediately after house no. 59A down Palmers Avenue. At the end keep forward into the bushes, cross the footbridge, go through a kissing-gate and turn left over the grass. At the far end keep forward along the track, passing another footbridge on the left, and in a few yards fork right up to the station car-park.

Walk 21
South Kirkby

Length of walk 6.06 miles (9.75 km), of which 2.49 miles (4 km) is Wakefield Way. The walk starts and finishes at Howell Wood Country Park car-park.

By bus: The 211 Doncaster-South Elmsall-Brierley-Grimethorpe-Barnsley *(hourly) passes the access road to Avenue Farm and Howell Wood Country Park (Burnt Wood Lane). Walk down to the car-park.*

By car: Howell Wood is signposted off Common Road, the road from Brierley to South Kirkby, about 600 yards east of the B6273 Hemsworth-Great Houghton road, down the access road to Avenue Farm, Burnt Wood Lane. Drive down the access road to the car-park.

Enter the car-park, turn right and walk to the far end, there taking the path in the right hand corner, keeping as close to the right hand edge of the wood as you can. Cross a beck by a footbridge and follow the path forward and uphill. At a fork keep right on the path closer to the edge of the wood. After a time the path bends left to reach a cross track by a bench. Turn right. Pass to the right of a large open grassy area. Cross a barrier in a high wire fence, here leaving the Country Park. When you reach a crossing, where a footpath comes in from the field on the right, keep straight on and follow the path close to the edge of the wood until it bears right to leave the wood in the top right hand corner.

Immediately you are faced with a fork: the right hand branch leads in a few yards to a tarmac road, Howell Lane; take the left hand branch, which leads to the corner of a field. Bear left here to follow the edge of the wood on your left. At the next corner of the wood turn half right across the large field, heading for some trees on the far side. At these trees a gap in the hedge leads to steps down to a track. Bear right over the field to Howell House Farm, cross a stile and the farm access road *(loose dogs might be a problem here)* and climb the bank to a kissing-gate.

Turn left and walk down the edge of the field with buildings on your left to the next stile, then on down the edge of the next field to a stone step-stile into the wood. A faint path leads forward, soon bearing right, crossing a broad cross path and dropping to a footbridge. Climb into the next field. The right of way goes diagonally left over the field to the top corner, but you may find a tractor track, intended to represent the path, heading first straight up the field and then turning left to the corner. At the hedge corner turn left, keeping the hedge on your left, for the short distance to the next

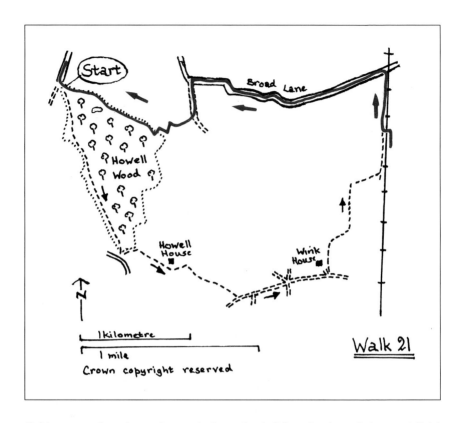

field corner, then keep forward along the left hand edge of the next field with the old hedge to your left, passing under the power lines a short distance to the right of one of the pylons.

When you reach a clear cross track, Top Lane, turn left along it. *Clayton village is over to the right. This elevated track provides good views to the left.* Keep forward, ignoring tracks and paths to left and right, and when you reach a large open space, the junction of several tracks, again keep straight forward. Shortly a wooden fence begins on both sides of the track and you reach the entrance to Wink House Farm on the left. Cross the stile in the fence on the corner and turn left along the edge of the field. Leaving Wink House to your left, walk the length of this field to a stile by a gate in the fence ahead. From the stile old paving stones lead forward for a short distance across the next field. Where they end, keep forward, and soon you will see the next stile to the right of a gate in the fence ahead. Cross it and bear right down the right hand edge of the field. When you reach a broad track coming through the hedge on your right, keep forward down it.

Follow the track down through the fields to a wood. *Here you enter Wakefield District.* The next section can be excessively muddy. After about 60 yards fork right along another track, almost exactly underneath the power lines. Shortly after passing to the right of a large pylon, and with the embankment of the Wakefield-Moorthorpe-Sheffield railway ahead, turn left on a track of much better quality. After a time ignore a track coming in from the right through a railway bridge. **Here you join the Wakefield Way. Follow your track to a road, cross and turn left along the footway, which however soon ends. Follow this road for almost a mile. After several bends the road descends very gently to a right hand bend followed by a left hand bend. Continue as far as the next right hand bend, there turning left along a track (signposted as a public bridleway).**

When you reach a point where the track bends left and a footpath forks off right, follow this, along the right hand edge of a field. It is a permissive path to Howell Wood. Where the hedge on the right ends, keep forward along the field boundary, at the end of the field turn left with the path, and follow it down to the wood. Here turn right and follow the path along the edge of the wood until a footbridge on the left gives access to the wood. At the junction of paths take the one furthest right, closest to the edge of the wood. You are now in Howell Wood Country Park. Keep always on the path nearest the edge of the wood, at one point ignoring a very clear path forking left.

At another point you have to descend some steps, cross a beck, then climb more steps to the bank of a small lake. Bear right round this, but soon fork right away from it to pass through a yew wood and return to the car-park. The Wakefield Way continues up the access road. *[To continue with the route of the WW, jump to p.84]*

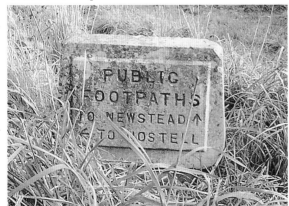

old waymark on the Newstead-Ryhill path (page 89)

Walk 22
Hemsworth

7.46 miles (12 km), of which 3.88 miles (6.25 km) is Wakefield Way.

By bus: 223 Wakefield-Hemsworth-S.Elmsall (hourly), 246 Pontefract-Barnsley, 247 Upton-Barnsley, 248/249 Pontefract-Upton, 496/498 Wakefield-S.Elmsall (every 15 mins) to the stop on the B6422 Hemsworth-S.Kirkby road just before the Hemsworth bypass. The walk starts at the car-park beside the bypass.

By car: There is a car-park at the junction of the B6422 Hemsworth-S.Kirkby road and the Hemsworth bypass. Park here.

Leave the car-park and turn left along the signposted bridleway, running parallel to the bypass. At the next roundabout cross straight over into the continuation of the path to the left of a large pylon. Follow the path all the way to the Brierley roundabout at the end of the bypass. Again cross straight over and take the signposted bridleway opposite. Soon the path passes through the hedge on the right and turns left. On leaving the next field, cross straight over a track to take the clear path opposite. Far below on the right a disused railway track emerges from the Brierley tunnel. The path is clear to the next road. Here the Wakefield Way turns right towards South Hiendley, *[To continue with the route of the WW, jump to p.86]* but we turn left along the footway.

On reaching the T-junction (A628) cross straight over to the footpath which starts behind the concrete barrier. At the end of this pleasant hedged path turn right and follow the wall on the right to a road in Brierley. Turn right, but where the road bends right at the post office, turn left along Cliff Lane. At the end of the tarmac ignore Cliff Close on the left and a track on the right: go through the kissing-gate and follow the paved path with a hedge on the left. *There is a fine view right.* When the paving ends, bear slightly right to follow the path down the left hand edge of the field. Ignore a track forking off right, after which your path is broader. Just before you reach the last house on the left, ignore a path forking right over the field, and immediately after the last house pass through a barrier, ignore another barrier on the right and turn left to the road.

Cross diagonally left to the stile by the gate opposite and follow the path forward with the remains of a fence on the right. When the fence bends right, stay with it, and when it bends right again, still keep with it. When it makes its last bend right and heads towards school buildings,

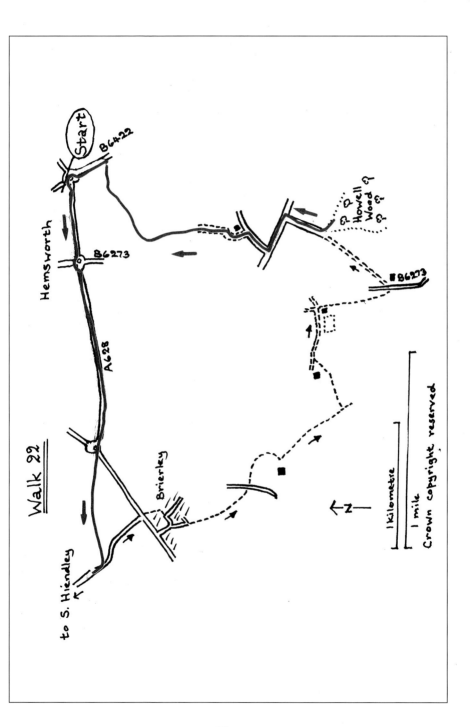

Walk 22

Start

B6422

Hemsworth

B6273

A628

Howell Wood

B6273

Brierley

to S. Hiendley

N

1 Kilometre
1 mile

Crown copyright reserved

83

bear left away from it, across the field, to a stile in the fence ahead. Cross and keep ahead for 15 yards, then turn sharp left on a clear path which passes a couple of benches and descends gently, then makes a sharp right hand bend and leads along parallel to the valley on the left.

At a fork keep left and drop to cross the beck by a footbridge. Keep straight forward up through the wood, soon bearing right on a path which climbs gently just inside the wood.

At the end of the wood cross the stile and follow the left hand edge of the field. Cross the makeshift stile into the next field and keep following the edge. Pass round another metal barrier ahead and turn left, immediately ignoring a path forking left into the next field and heading towards a detached house in the distance. The path follows the left hand edge of this field, soon becoming a track. Look out for the point where a footpath forks right off the track into the field, then continues parallel to the track with a hedge on the left. The path leads to a gate in the hedge. Pass through - the detached house is along to the left - and turn right along the track.

Pass to the left of a reservoir and a house, and at a crossing of tracks turn right. Follow this track along the right hand edge of a very large field to the next road (B6273) at Burntwood Hall. Cross the road and turn half left along a track. In a few yards, at a junction of tracks, keep straight forward along the grassy track (Burnt Wood Lane). When you reach the entrance to the Howell Wood Country Park car-park on the right, the surface becomes tarmac. **Here you re-join the Wakefield Way. Keep forward up the road. At the T-junction turn left and at the next road junction fork right.**

Immediately before a large detached house on the left turn left along a track (Hague Lane). *Soon there are extensive views to South Kirkby, South Elmsall, Upton and round to Hemsworth.* **Where the track ends, a footpath forks right down through trees. On emerging from the trees, turn left, soon bearing right down the field edge with a beck and wood on the left. When the beck you have been following is joined by Hague Hall Beck coming from the left, turn right, and keeping the beck and the trees on your left, follow this attractive path to the next road (B6422). Cross the road and turn left up the footway. On reaching the Hague Hall roundabout on the Hemsworth bypass, cross straight over the main road and follow the Hemsworth road for a short distance, before crossing it to the signposted bridleway** *[To continue with the route of the WW, jump back to p.82]* and the car-park from which you started.

Walk 23
South Hiendley

Length of walk 3.42 miles (5.5 km), of which 1.55 miles (2.5 km) is Wakefield Way. The walk starts and finishes by the village pond at South Hiendley Common.

By bus: 195 Wakefield-Ryhill-South Hiendley-Hemsworth (half-hourly) to South Hiendley Common.

By car: Park considerately by the village pond at South Hiendley Common.

Take the track with the pond on your right, but almost immediately fork right off it to cross a clapper bridge and follow the path up towards the grassy hill of High Common. Before a major fork in the path fork left on a path which is not very clear, which soon bears left to re-cross the beck. Presently you cross a stile and are walking along the left hand edge of a field. After a time the path forks left to cross a stile out of the field and follow a fence on the right. Cross a track and keep forward along a hedged path. Cross a stile and walk forward to a junction. Cross the South Hiendley School access drive and keep forward with the school to your right into a fenced footpath.

A stile gives access to the main road: turn right. Pass the mini-roundabout and at the next fork keep right. Ignore Braemar Croft on the right (twice!). At the top of the hill the road bends left: at the fork keep left along the tarmac lane. *Running along a ridge, this lane offers quite extensive views to right and left, including much of the route traversed by the Wakefield Way.* **On reaching a derelict factory, take the road on the left, here leaving the Wakefield Way,** *[To continue with the route of the WW, jump to p.89]* and at the main road cross and turn right. In a few yards turn left down steps onto a disused railway track.

After a time the track bends right. Cross a bridge over another disused railway track below you, then fork right to descend to this second track and turn right along it, passing under the bridge you have just crossed. After a time you pass under a road bridge - this can be very muddy - and climb to resume your route along the old track. After a time the old track drops into a dip and meets a cross track, yet another former railway line. Turn left along it. Ignore a stile on the right, and a short distance further ignore a path forking right into the wood. A little further along ignore another path forking right. At one point a bridge has gone, so you have the easy crossing of a beck on makeshift stepping stones. A bit further along leave the track, which becomes very wet, by crossing a plank footbridge on the right. The path bends left with a fence on the right. Pass the remains of a stile - a footpath crosses the field on the right - and continue along the top of the embankment.

Remain on the top of the embankment until a path comes up from the track down on the left, and your path swings right briefly away from the old trackbed, before returning to the top of the embankment. The path is less clear now, as you approach the only major obstacle on the route, the crossing of the valley of Hemp Dike, which comes in from the right. Stay with the path and cross the valley on tussocks of grass, climb the other side and resume your former direction, with the old trackbed once more below on your left. The clear path soon leads to the road at Frickley Bridge. Turn left to cross the bridge, **here re-joining the Wakefield Way.**

Having entered South Hiendley, at the end of the first row of houses on the left, opposite the first street on the right, a footpath sign points left. Follow the path as far as the football nets, then turn right and head for the right of the isolated house, crossing a track just past the second set of goalposts. Having crossed the access drive to the house, the path is clear ahead, parallel to the road down on the right. Here you are crossing Low Common. Cross a footbridge, rejoin the road, cross it and turn left to return to your starting point. *[To continue with the route of the WW, jump back to the previous page]*

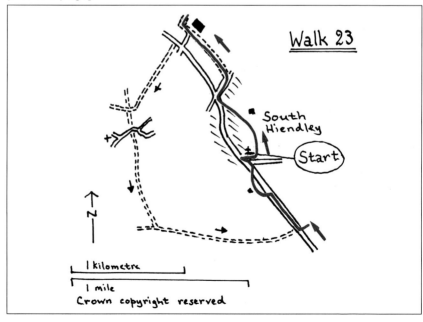

Walk 23

South
Hiendley

Start

1 kilometre

1 mile

Crown copyright reserved

86

Walk 24
South Hiendley, Havercroft and Wintersett

Length of walk 5.9 miles (9.5 km), of which 3.11 miles (5 km) is Wakefield Way. The walk starts and finishes at Anglers Country Park, where there are an information centre, café and toilets.

By bus: *195/196 Wakefield-Ryhill-Hemsworth, 197 Wakefield-Ryhill-Newstead to Wintersett, then pick up the walk at [*] below.*

By car: *Anglers Country Park and the Waterton Countryside Discovery Centre are well signposted from surrounding roads. The car-park is on Haw Park Lane (GR 375 153).*

Leave the car-park at Anglers Country Park and turn right along the road, immediately ignoring a fork left to the West Riding Sailing Club. At the next fork, where the right hand branch is barred to motor traffic by a locked gate, go left, in a few yards ignoring a minor track forking left. Just after the track makes a right hand bend, keep left at the next fork on a path which climbs onto the embankment of Wintersett Reservoir. Soon you pass Cold Hiendley Reservoir down on the right. *Both reservoirs were built in the 19th century to supply water to the Barnsley Canal.* Cross a concrete bridge and continue along the raised path.

At the next fork keep right, down off the embankment onto a path across the middle of a field. On the far side turn left and follow the path to a road. Turn left along it. Where the road makes a sharp turn left, ignore the bridleway to the right and take the footpath straight ahead across the field. At the far side cross over a former railway track and follow the path over the next field to a cross path. Turn left along it, *here joining the Barnsley Boundary Walk, at this point making an excursion into Wakefield territory.* In just over 100 yards turn right to cross a sleeper footbridge, and walk straight across the next field, aiming just to the left of the first large metal pylon.

Join the next road at a junction and take Church Lane straight ahead. At the next crossroads keep straight on (signposted Hemsworth), still on Church Lane. There is a bench here. After about 250 yards there are a layby on the left and two metal gates a short distance apart. Go through the barrier by the second gate onto a disused railway track. *The tower of Felkirk Church is visible half right.* After a time cross a large stony open space, after which keep right at a fork. Cross a bridge over another disused railway line down below and follow the track up to the next road. Cross and turn right, but take the first road on the left.

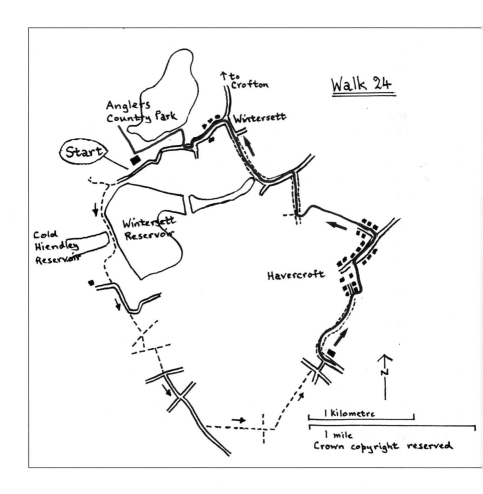

Walk 24

to Crofton

Anglers Country Park

Wintersett

Start

Wintersett Reservoir

Cold Hiendley Reservoir

Havercroft

N

1 Kilometre

1 mile
Crown copyright reserved

Just before you reach a disused factory there is a T-junction. Turn left, here joining the Wakefield Way. Follow the tarmac lane as it turns right, ignoring footpaths across the field ahead. In the wood ignore a track forking right. On reaching the houses at Havercroft, pass through a barrier, in a few yards forking right through another barrier along a tarmac footpath. Follow this path, which soon widens, to the main road (B6428) through Havercroft, crossing grass to reach it. Cross the road and turn right. At the top of the hill turn left along the last street before the de-restriction sign.

Where the houses end, head to the right of a track leading to a motor repair shop, and passing through a kissing gate immediately keep left at a fork and walk along the left hand edge of the field. You are joined by a track coming in over your right shoulder, and 20 yards further on the track divides. Keep right on a track between hedges. Sometimes a track, sometimes a path, this eventually descends to cross a dismantled railway line. Turn right up this and follow it to the next road. Turn left along the left hand verge.

Where the road bends left at the start of the 30 m.p.h. limit, take the track forking right (bridleway). Cross yet another disused railway line by passing under a missing bridge. An upright stone slab marks the beginning of a pleasant green lane. You emerge at a bend in the Wintersett to Wragby road: continue straight ahead towards Wintersett. At the T-junction in the village turn left [*] to pass the Anglers' Retreat pub. Take the next lane on the right, signposted for Anglers Country Park, but after about 100 yards turn right through a signposted gap in the hedge, pass through a squeeze stile and immediately keep right at the fork along a path which leads to the lake. You can then enjoy the delights of this country park, perhaps by making an anti-clockwise circuit of the lake. Or just turn left and follow the lakeside path to the visitor centre and the end of the Wakefield Way.

The **Ramblers' Association,** a registered charity, is an organisation dedicated to the preservation and care of the countryside and its network of footpaths, and to helping people to appreciate and enjoy them.

Through its Central Office the Ramblers' Association lobbies and campaigns for more effective legislation to achieve

the preservation and improvement of the footpath network

better access to the countryside

the preservation and enhancement for the benefit of the public of the beauty of the countryside.

Since its formation in 1935 the Ramblers' Association has grown into a powerful campaigning organisation with a membership of 140,000.

The Association relies on many volunteers working at Area and Local Group level to help achieve these objectives.

The **West Riding Area** is one of the 51 Areas of the Ramblers' Association which cover England, Wales and Scotland. It includes the whole of West Yorkshire and parts of North Yorkshire around Selby, York, Harrogate, Ripon, Skipton and Settle, as well as the southern part of the Yorkshire Dales National Park. The Area has over 4,000 members and is divided into 14 Local Groups. The West Riding Area's website is **www.ramblersyorkshire.org**

The **Local Groups** carry out the work of the Ramblers' Association by keeping an eye on the state of footpaths in their area and monitoring proposed closures and diversions.

They put pressure on their Local Authority to take action to remove obstructions and re-instate footpaths after ploughing.

They do practical work of footpath clearance and waymarking, and can erect stiles and footbridges.

Where the Local Authority has set up consultation procedures, e.g. Footpath Forums, the Local Group will normally send a representative.

Many Local Groups produce their own programme of walks.

Regular walks are a very important part of Ramblers' activities. As well as ensuring that local footpaths are used, they provide healthy recreation and the opportunity to make new friends.

If you use and enjoy the footpath network, please help us to protect it, by joining the Ramblers' Association. For further information contact The Ramblers' Association, 2nd Floor, Camelford House, 87-90 Albert Embankment, London SE1 7TW (Tel.: 020 7339 8500, Fax.: 020 7339 8501; e-mail: ramblers@london.ramblers.org.uk).

Or visit our website: **www.ramblers.org.uk**

RECORD OF THE WAKEFIELD WAY

Date	Place	Km	Km total	Start time	Finish time	Comments
	Anglers Country Park	0	0			
	Walton	3	3			
	Old railway bridge near Notton	5¾	8¾			
	Woolley	6¾	15½			
	Junction in wood after Bretton Park	8¾	24¼			
	Overton	5	29¼			
	Horbury Bridge	8	37¼			

Date	Place	Km	Km total	Start time	Finish time	Comments
	Chickenley	5¼	42½			
	Gawthorpe	2¾	45¼			
	Lindale Hill	3½	48¾			
	Outwood	5¼	54			
	Stanley	6½	60½			
	Ramsdens Bridge	1½	62			
	Altofts	3	65			
	Castleford	7	72			
	Pontefract	7	79			

Date	Place	Km	Km total	Start time	Finish time	Comments
	East Hardwick	8	87			
	Burnhill Bridge	2¼	89¼			
	Upton	6	95¼			
	South Elmsall	4½	99¾			
	railway tunnel	3	102¾			
	Howell Wood Country Park	4	106¾			
	Frickley Bridge	6¼	113			
	derelict factory	2½	115½			
	Anglers Country Park	5	120½			

RECORD OF WALKS COMPLETED

Date	Walk	Start time	Finish time	Comments
	Anglers Country Park and The Heronry			
	Walton and Newmillerdam			
	Notton and Woolley			
	Woolley to Bretton Hall			
	Bank Wood and Stony Cliffe Wood			
	Horbury Bridge, Netherton ... Middlestown			
	Horbury Bridge to Chickenley			
	Gawthorpe, Chidswell ... Earlsheaton			
	Gawthorpe to Kirkhamgate			

Date	Walk	Start time	Finish time	Comments
	Kirkhamgate to Outwood Station			
	Outwood Station to Stanley			
	Stanley			
	Stanley Ferry to Altofts and Kirkthorpe			
	Normanton Station to Castleford Station			
	Castleford Station to Pontefract Bus Station			
	Pontefract Bus Station to East Hardwick			
	East Hardwick and Ackworth			
	Thorpe Audlin and Upton			

Date	Walk	Start time	Finish time	Comments
	South and North Elmsall and Wrangbrook			
	South Elmsall			
	South Kirkby			
	Hemsworth			
	South Hiendley			
	South Hiendley, Havercroft, Wintersett			